S. HRG. 113–36

U.S. POLICY TOWARD NORTH KOREA

HEARING

BEFORE THE

COMMITTEE ON FOREIGN RELATIONS
UNITED STATES SENATE

ONE HUNDRED THIRTEENTH CONGRESS

FIRST SESSION

MARCH 7, 2013

Printed for the use of the Committee on Foreign Relations

Available via the World Wide Web: http://www.gpo.gov/fdsys/

U.S. GOVERNMENT PRINTING OFFICE

81–468 PDF   WASHINGTON : 2013

For sale by the Superintendent of Documents, U.S. Government Printing Office
Internet: bookstore.gpo.gov   Phone: toll free (866) 512–1800; DC area (202) 512–1800
Fax: (202) 512–2104   Mail: Stop IDCC, Washington, DC 20402–0001

(II)

CONTENTS

U.S. POLICY TOWARD NORTH KOREA

THURSDAY, MARCH 7, 2013

U.S. SENATE,
COMMITTEE ON FOREIGN RELATIONS,
Washington, DC.

The committee met, pursuant to notice, at 10:01 a.m., in room SD–419, Dirksen Senate Office Building, Hon. Robert Menendez (chairman of the committee) presiding.

Present: Senators Menendez, Cardin, Shaheen, Udall, Murphy, Kaine, Corker, Rubio, Johnson, Flake, McCain, and Paul.

OPENING STATEMENT OF HON. ROBERT MENENDEZ, U.S SENATOR FROM NEW JERSEY

The CHAIRMAN. Good morning. This meeting of the Senate Foreign Relations Committee will come to order.

This being the first hearing of this new term, it could not be a more timely hearing. Recent developments in North Korea, most notably, the February 12, 2013, nuclear test and the December 12, 2012, missile tests, highlight the growing threat that North Korea poses to the United States, our allies and friends in the region, and the increasing dangers of severe instability on the Korean Peninsula. Given this growing set of circumstances, I believe the committee needs to take a close look at current United States policy toward North Korea, evaluate its effectiveness, and identify any midcourse corrections or new measures that are required to get our North Korea policy right.

I understand that as we convene this hearing, this morning, that in New York the United Nations Security Council is sitting down to consider a resolution that imposes additional sanctions on North Korea. This new Security Council resolution, based on a United States-China draft, includes tough new sanctions intended to impede North Korea's ability to develop further its illicit nuclear and ballistic missile programs. These sanctions include targeting the illicit activities of North Korean diplomatic personnel, North Korean banking relationships, illicit transfers of bulk cash, and new travel restrictions.

I think that these actions are a step in the right direction and very much in keeping with the sort of approach that the ranking member, Senator Corker, and I called for in the North Korea Nonproliferation and Accountability Act of 2013, which the Senate passed on February 25.

And I congratulate the administration on moving things forward so effectively at the United Nations.

(1)

But I also believe that we need to do more to better determine how the United States can combine effective sanctions and military countermeasures with strong and realistic diplomacy aimed at North Korea and at China—and with the clear goal of North Korea's abandonment of its nuclear programs.

North Korea yesterday made what I consider to be, of course, an absurd threat of a "preemptive nuclear attack" to destroy the strongholds of the "aggressors" in response to the action that the United States, China, and others are seeking at the United Nations.

There should be no doubt about our determination, willingness, and capability to neutralize and counter any threat that North Korea may present. I do not think that the regime in Pyongyang wants to commit suicide but, as they must surely know, that would be the result of any attack on the United States.

But even as we think about potential measures and actions necessary to safeguard the United States and our allies, there should also be no doubt about our determination to work with the international community through peaceful diplomatic means to achieve a denuclearized Korean Peninsula.

Today it is estimated that North Korea has accumulated between 20 and 40 kilograms of plutonium, enough perhaps for six to eight nuclear weapons. It has now conducted three nuclear explosive tests. It has developed a modern gas centrifuge uranium enrichment program to go along with its plutonium stockpile, and it is seeking to develop the capability to mate a nuclear warhead to an intercontinental ballistic missile.

Taken together, these developments present a growing danger that North Korea may well become a small nuclear power, a scenario which, while bad enough on its own, could well have additional dangerous effects if it leads other nations in the region to reconsider their own commitments to nonproliferation.

Moreover, there is also the continuing danger of further conventional military provocation from North Korea that results in a serious military clash between North and South and the potential for unintended escalation that could draw in the United States and China and result in a dangerous confrontation on the peninsula.

And beyond these security concerns, there are also the ongoing questions about human rights and the lot of the North Korean people. Security concerns may be our most important priority on the peninsula, but they are not our only priority.

It has now been a little over a year since Kim Jong-un took power amid speculation that this transition could lead to a period of instability inside the North, perhaps even leading to collapse. Yet, that instability does not appear to have materialized. Although, of course, we can never be sure about what the future is in North Korea, by all appearances Kim has asserted control over the military and strengthened party institutions, and contrary to some media hype focus on his education in Switzerland, he has not proved to be a reformer. It is unclear whether he has any objectives other than maintaining tight control of his political and economic system.

Above all else, North Korea clearly represents a real and growing threat to national security interests and therefore deserves our close attention. In time, if its present course remains unaltered, North Korea could pose a direct threat to the United States.

Today North Korea certainly poses a growing threat to our allies and to American forces in the region. It also threatens to undermine the international nonproliferation regime, particularly as its arsenal grows, by spreading its threat to other countries through a transfer of nuclear technology and materials. We know, for example, that North Korea has made efforts to proliferate nuclear technology in the past, building a plutonium separation plant in Syria which Israel destroyed by bombing it before its completion, and we know that there is a long history of North Korean-Iranian military cooperation.

I hope that this hearing, as well as a continuing dialogue with the administration on this issue, will help us explore several key questions that are critical to informing our future policy toward North Korea. Does North Korea pursue a nuclear weapons program as a deterrent for defensive purposes, or does it pursue such a program as part of a policy intended to reunify the peninsula by force? Could the current regime ever conceive of parting with its nuclear capability, or does it view these weapons as essential tools as deterrence against others to continue its hold on power? Getting these answers right will be critical to determining if there is hope for diplomacy or if a different approach is necessary.

It is also important to note the coming power of a new South Korean administration led by President Park at this difficult time. We offer her our congratulations on her inauguration last week. There is no basis for successfully dealing with the North absent a solid foundation for policy rooted in the United States-Republic of Korea alliance. With President Park's inauguration, we have an opportunity to consult and work closely with a close ally to chart our future course in dealing with North Korea.

And finally, we need to consider how recent transitions in other countries in the region, including our close ally, Japan, as well as China, may present new opportunities in building a more effective approach to dealing with Pyongyang.

Whatever one's views on the various policy efforts of the past two decades, and what has worked and what has not worked and why, there can be little question that these efforts have failed to end North Korea's nuclear or missile programs, failed to reduce the threat posed to our allies, and failed to lead to greater security in the region. But I am hopeful that today's hearing and the conversation we start today may help us get to a place where 20 years from now we can look back at successfully having ended North Korea's nuclear and missile programs, and having built greater stability and security on the peninsula and throughout the Asia-Pacific region.

Let me call upon the distinguished ranking member, Senator Corker, for his comments.

OPENING STATEMENT OF HON. BOB CORKER,
U.S. SENATOR FROM TENNESSEE

Senator CORKER. Thank you, Mr. Chairman, for this timely hearing.

And welcome, Ambassador Davies. We thank you for being here. I look forward to hearing from you today, along with our panel of expert witnesses later this morning.

North Korea's nuclear weapons program, missile program, and proliferation activities pose a threat to the United States national security interests.

Over several decades, United States policymakers have attempted to influence North Korea's behavior through an array of deterrent tools, including inducements and punitive measures. U.S. officials have used diplomacy, energy assistance, financial sanctions, and counterproliferation tools, including proactive interdiction activities. Despite the varying combinations of tools, the United States has failed to persuade the North Korean regime to abandon its nuclear weapons program.

We know that North Korea continues to engage in a range of illicit and proliferation-related activities to generate hard currency to support the regime. Simultaneously, the situation for the North Korean people has continued to deteriorate with rampant human rights abuses, the continued expansion of North Korean prison camps, and some analysts estimate they may hold as many as 200,000 political prisoners.

In addition, China continues to serve as North Korea's primary benefactor, accounting for nearly 60 percent of all North Korean trade. Beijing remains Pyongyang's main source of food and fuel. United States policymakers have not been able to persuade China that the costs of Beijing's continued support for North Korea far outweigh the perceived benefits. It is clear that we must redouble our efforts in that regard.

I recognize that North Korea is a complex policy conundrum and that there is no silver bullet solution. Yet, after nearly 20 years of unsuccessful policies by successive administrations, it seems logical to me that we ought to undertake a comprehensive review of our North Korean strategy, including harnessing new tools to try to crack the North Korean policy nut.

That is why I worked with Senator Menendez and other members of this committee to move forward with the North Korean Nonproliferation and Accountability Act, S. 298, which would require the administration to review our approach to North Korea. Undertaking such a review does not require abandoning diplomatic efforts nor terminating sanctions. However, it necessitates that we redouble efforts to think outside the box.

In recent months, it has become increasingly clear to me that U.S. policymakers ought to pay closer attention to the nonmilitary aspects of deterrence, including efforts to weaken and debilitate the North Korean regime. In particular, we ought to do more to expose the North's brutality toward its own citizens as a means to influence the Kim regime.

We also should promote the flow of information to the North Korean people, including through our own Radio Free Asia broadcasts.

However, do not mistake my interests in the nonmilitary aspects of deterrence as a call to abandon the military and security aspects of our overall North Korea policy. I firmly believe that a robust United States nuclear deterrent is essential to United States security and it remains critical to maintaining our security commitments to allies in the Asia-Pacific, including Japan and South Korea. I know that Ambassador Joseph will speak to the importance of our nuclear deterrent later during this hearing.

Ambassador Davies, I do look forward to hearing from you regarding the administration's strategy for confronting North Korea, including our efforts this week at the Security Council on a new sanctions resolution.

In addition, I look forward to hearing from you and all of our expert witnesses about our capabilities to deter North Korean provocations, options to elicit enhanced Chinese cooperation, and opportunities to improve the lives of the North Korean people.

Thank you, Mr. Chairman.

The CHAIRMAN. Thank you, Senator Corker.

Today's two panels pull together some of the top decisionmakers on North Korean policy from the current and several previous administrations. They represent decades of experience, following North Korea from both in and outside the Government, and can bear witness to years of both progress and setbacks in our policy. And I can think of no better group to help analyze what has worked and what has not, and I fully expect they may hold, in some cases, quite different views in this regard. That is only natural considering the critical importance and extraordinary complexity of addressing North Korea, and I would view simple answers with considerable skepticism. So we are going to look forward to this discussion.

We start off with the distinguished Ambassador Glyn Davies. He has served as the Special Representative of the Secretary of State for North Korea Policy since January 2012. He oversees U.S. involvement in the six-party talks process, as well as aspects of our security, political, economic, human rights, and humanitarian assistance policy regarding North Korea. He is a career member of the Senior Foreign Service, served previously as the Permanent Representative of the United States to the International Atomic Energy Agency and the U.N. office in Vienna, as well as the Principal Deputy Assistant Secretary of State in the Bureau of East Asian and Pacific Affairs and Executive Secretary of the National Security Council staff. So an extraordinary wealth of knowledge. We welcome you to the committee and look forward to your testimony.

STATEMENT OF HON. GLYN T. DAVIES, SPECIAL REPRESENTATIVE FOR NORTH KOREA POLICY, U.S. DEPARTMENT OF STATE, WASHINGTON, DC

Ambassador DAVIES. Well, thank you very much, Chairman Menendez and Senator Corker and members of the committee, for inviting me to testify today on United States policy toward North Korea or, as it is also known, the Democratic People's Republic of Korea.

North Korea's February 12 announcement of its third nuclear test and its subsequent threats to conduct even more follow-on measures are only the latest in a long line of reminders that the DPRK's nuclear weapons and ballistic missile programs and proliferation activities pose serious threats to U.S. national security, to regional security in the Asia-Pacific, and to the global nonproliferation regime.

Pyongyang continues to violate its international obligations and commitments, including to denuclearize. Its human rights record remains deplorable. Its economy is stagnant. Its people are impoverished. It pours significant sums into nuclear and ballistic missile programs that are forbidden by the United Nations.

The DPRK has consistently failed to take advantage of the alternatives available. The United States has offered Pyongyang an improved relationship, provided North Korea demonstrates a willingness to fulfill its denuclearization commitments and address other concerns. The DPRK rebuffed these offers and instead responded with a series of provocations that drew widespread international condemnation.

North Korea again brazenly defied the international community on April 13, 2012, and again on December 12, 2012, with long-range missile launches, in flagrant violation of U.N. Security Council resolutions and in the face of united calls from the international community to desist. Some 60 countries and international organizations issued statements criticizing the December launch.

The DPRK's February 12 announcement of a nuclear test, which Pyongyang proclaimed was targeted against the United States of America, represents an even bolder threat to national security, the stability of the regime, and the global nonproliferation regime. The international response has been unprecedented. Over 80 countries and international organizations from all corners of the world have condemned the tests.

We are working with the international community to make clear that North Korea's nuclear test has costly consequences. In adopting Resolution 2087 in January after the December launch, the U.N. Security Council pledged to take significant action in the event of a nuclear test. We are working hard at the United Nations Security Council to make good on that pledge, and as you noted, Mr. Chairman, that is occurring even as we speak and we are hoping that the council adopts the resolution that the United States put forward. The Security Council will deliver a credible and strong response that further impedes the growth of North Korea's nuclear weapons and ballistic missiles program and its ability to engage in proliferation activities.

The resolution today that we tabled builds upon, strengthens, and significantly expands the scope of the strong U.N. sanctions already in place. The sanctions contained in this draft resolution will significantly impede North Korea's ability to proceed in developing its nuclear and missile programs and significantly expand the scope of the tools the United Nations has available to counter these North Korean developments.

We are also strengthening our close coordination with our six-party partners and our regional allies, and through a whole-of-government approach, working closely with our partners in the Department of Defense and other agencies, we will take the steps necessary to defend ourselves and our allies, particularly the Republic of Korea and Japan.

Effective, targeted multilateral and national sanctions will remain a vital component of our effort to impede the DPRK from advancing its nuclear weapons and ballistic missile programs and its proliferation activities. We continue to exercise national authorities to sanction North Korean entities, individuals, and those that support them in facilitating programs that threaten the American people. Most recently on January 24, the Departments of State and the Treasury designated a number of North Korean individuals and entities under Executive Order 13–382, which targets actors involved in the proliferation of weapons of mass destruction and their supporters. We will continue to take national measures as appropriate.

Sanctions are not a punitive measure, but rather a tool to impede the development of North Korea's nuclear and missile programs and its proliferation-related exports, as well as to make clear the costs of North Korea's defiance of its international obligations, and working toward our end game will require an openness to meaningful dialogue with the DPRK.

We remain committed to authentic and credible negotiations to implement the September 2005 joint statement of the six-party talks and to bring North Korea into compliance with its international obligations through irreversible steps leading to denuclearization.

The United States will not engage in talks for talks' sake. Authentic and credible talks will first require a serious, meaningful change in North Korea's priorities, demanding that Pyongyang is prepared to meet its commitments and obligations on denuclearization.

This leads to a few important other principles. First and foremost, the United States will not accept North Korea as a nuclear-armed state. We will not reward the DPRK for the absence of bad behavior. We will not compensate the DPRK merely for returning to dialogue. We will not tolerate North Korea provoking its neighbors. We have made clear that U.S.-DPRK relations cannot fundamentally improve without sustained improvement in inter-Korean relations and in human rights. These positions will not change.

In the meantime, active United States diplomacy on North Korea on a wide range of issues continues. Close coordination with our valued treaty allies, the ROK and Japan, remain absolutely central to our approach.

We have also expanded our engagement by developing new dialogues on North Korea with key global actors who have joined the rising chorus of voices calling on the DPRK to comply with its international obligations.

China, however, does remain central to altering North Korea's cost calculus and close United States-China consultations on North Korea will remain for us a key focus of diplomatic efforts in the weeks and months ahead.

While denuclearization remains an essential goal of United States policy, so too does the welfare of North Korea's nearly 25 million people, the vast majority of whom bear the brunt of the government's decision to perpetuate an unsustainable, self-impoverishing, military-first policy. Improving human rights conditions is an integral part of our overall North Korea policy, and how the

DPRK addresses human rights will have a significant impact on prospects for improved U.S.-DPRK ties.

The entire world is increasingly taking note of the grave, widespread, and systematic human rights violations in the DPRK and demanding action. The United Nations High Commissioner for Human Rights Navi Pillay has called for an in-depth international inquiry to document abuses. We support this call, and next week, my colleague, Special Envoy for North Korea Human Rights Issues Robert King, will travel to Geneva to attend the United Nations Human Rights Council's 22nd session where he will call attention to North Korea's human rights record and urge adoption of an enhanced mechanism of inquiry into the regime's abuses against the North Korean people.

Mr. Chairman, the Obama administration's dual-track policy of engagement and pressure toward the DPRK reflects a bipartisan recognition that only a policy of openness to dialogue when possible, combined with sustained, robust pressure through sanctions when necessary, can maximize prospects for progress in denuclearizing North Korea.

But genuine progress requires a fundamental shift in North Korea's strategic calculus. The DPRK leadership must choose between provocation or peace, isolation or integration. North Korea will not achieve security, economic prosperity, and integration into the international community while it pursues nuclear weapons, while it threatens its neighbors, while it tramples on international norms, abuses its own people, and refuses to fulfill its longstanding obligations and commitments.

The DPRK leadership in Pyongyang faces increasingly sharp choices, and we are working with our friends and allies to further sharpen these choices. If the North Korean regime is at all wise, it will reembark on a path to denuclearization for the benefit of the North Korean people, the Northeast Asian region, and the world.

Mr. Chairman, thank you again for this chance to appear before you today, and I am happy to try and address any questions you may have. Thank you, sir.

[The prepared statement of Ambassador Davies follows:]

PREPARED STATEMENT OF HON. GLYN T. DAVIES

Chairman Menendez, Senator Corker, and Members of the committee, thank you for inviting me to testify today on U.S. policy toward the Democratic People's Republic of Korea (DPRK).

Nearly 60 years have passed since the conclusion of the armistice that ended the hostilities of the Korean war, yet North Korea still persists as one of the thorniest challenges confronting the United States and the international community. Pyongyang's February 12 announcement of a third nuclear test—conducted in brazen defiance of the demands of the United Nations Security Council—and its subsequent threats to conduct even more follow-on "measures" are only the latest in a long line of reminders that the DPRK's nuclear weapons and ballistic missile programs and proliferation activities pose serious threats to U.S. national security, to regional security in the Asia-Pacific, and to the global nonproliferation regime.

Pyongyang continues to violate its international obligations and commitments, including to denuclearize. Its human rights record remains deplorable. Its economy is stagnant. Its people are impoverished. It pours significant sums into nuclear and ballistic missile programs that are forbidden by the United Nations. The leadership's choices are isolating North Korea from the international community. International outrage against North Korea and its provocative and threatening actions, meanwhile, continues to grow.

The DPRK has consistently failed to take advantage of the alternatives available. The United States offered—and has continued to offer—Pyongyang an improved relationship with the United States and integration into the international community, provided North Korea demonstrated a willingness to fulfill its denuclearization commitments and address other concerns. The DPRK rebuffed these offers and instead responded with a series of provocations that drew widespread international condemnation.

Pyongyang appeared prepared to enter a period of serious diplomatic engagement in mid-2011, and the United States responded with a proactive, nearly year-long diplomatic effort to push forward on denuclearization in a way that would lay the groundwork for improved bilateral relations. Starting in July 2011 and continuing over the next 10 months, the United States and the DPRK held three rounds of bilateral denuclearization talks on three continents. In our meetings, we worked to forge the conditions necessary for resuming the six-party talks, which had been stalled since 2008. Shortly after Kim Jong-un's assumption of power, we reached a modest but potentially important bilateral understanding announced on February 29, 2012.

Pyongyang announced its commitment to, among other things, a moratorium on nuclear tests, long-range missile launches, and all nuclear activity, including uranium enrichment activity, at the Yongbyon nuclear complex. North Korea also committed to allow International Atomic Energy Agency inspectors to return to Yongbyon to monitor the cessation of uranium enrichment and confirm the disablement of plutonium-related facilities there.

But just 16 days later, North Korea reneged on these commitments by announcing its intent to launch a satellite into orbit. Such launches use ballistic missile technology proscribed by multiple U.N. Security Council resolutions (UNSCRs), and we had made it abundantly clear during our negotiations that such a launch, even if characterized as a satellite launch, would be a deal-breaker. Pyongyang nevertheless conducted such a launch on April 13 and was greeted by deep international opprobrium. All five six-party partners—China, Russia, the United States, the Republic of Korea (ROK), and Japan—joined a long list of states publicly condemning Pyongyang's provocation. The U.N. Security Council unanimously issued a Presidential Statement condemning the act as a "serious violation" of UNSCRs 1718 and 1874, tightened existing sanctions, and made clear its commitment to "take action accordingly" in the event of another launch.

North Korea again brazenly defied the international community on December 12, 2012, with another long-range missile launch, again characterized by the DPRK as a satellite launch, in flagrant violation of U.N. Security Council Resolutions 1718 and 1874 and in the face of united public and private calls by the international community to desist. Over 60 countries and international organizations issued statements criticizing the launch. The U.N. Security Council unanimously adopted UNSCR 2087, which condemned the launch, further expanded the scope of sanctions on the DPRK, and promised "significant action" in the event of a future DPRK missile launch or nuclear test.

The DPRK's February 12 announcement of a nuclear test, which Pyongyang proclaimed was targeted against the United States, represents an even bolder threat to U.S. national security, the stability of the region, and the global nonproliferation regime. The international response has been unprecedented. Over 80 countries and international organizations from all corners of the world have decried the test. Many are speaking out against DPRK provocations for the first time. As the list continues to grow, it is increasingly clear that an international consensus is coalescing in opposition to North Korea's destabilizing activities.

We are working with the international community to make clear that North Korea's nuclear test has costly consequences. In adopting Resolution 2087 in January after the December launch, the U.N. Security Council pledged to take "significant action" in the event of a nuclear test; we are working hard at the U.N. Security Council to make good on that pledge. We are intensively engaged with our six-party partners, members of the U.N. Security Council, and other U.N. Member States on a strong and credible response by the international community.

China's support for firm action remains key, and we are deeply engaged with the Chinese in shaping an appropriate response. We are strengthening our close coordination with our six-party partners and regional allies. And—through a whole-of-government approach, working closely with our partners in the Department of Defense and other agencies—we will take the steps necessary to defend ourselves and our allies, particularly the ROK and Japan. We have reassured both Seoul and Tokyo, at the highest levels, of our commitment to extended deterrence through the U.S. nuclear umbrella, conventional capabilities, and missile defense.

North Korea's WMD, ballistic missile, conventional arms, and proliferation activities constitute a serious and unacceptable threat to U.S. national security, to say nothing of the integrity of the global nonproliferation regime, which many around the world have labored—over generations—to devise, nurture, and enforce. Effective, targeted multilateral and national sanctions will consequently remain a vital component of our efforts to impede the DPRK's efforts to advance its nuclear weapons and ballistic missile programs and proliferation activities. UNSCR 2087 was an important step forward in this regard. Combined with the measures in Resolutions 1718 and 1874, UNSCR 2087 further constricts North Korea's efforts to procure weapons components, send agents abroad, smuggle dual-use items, and make headway on its nuclear weapons and ballistic missile programs.

Full and transparent implementation of these resolutions by all U.N. Member States, including China, is critical. We are actively engaged with the international community to underscore the importance of full enforcement of these measures.

We also continue to exercise national authorities to sanction North Korean entities, individuals, and those that support them in facilitating programs that threaten the American people. Most recently, on January 24, the Departments of State and the Treasury designated a number of North Korean individuals and entities under Executive Order 13382, which targets actors involved in the proliferation of weapons of mass destruction and their supporters. The Department of State designated the Korean Committee for Space Technology—North Korea's space agency—and several officials directly involved in North Korea's April 2012 and December 2012 launches, which contributed to the DPRK's long-range ballistic missile development efforts. The Department of the Treasury designated several Beijing-based North Korean officials linked to the DPRK's Tanchon Commercial Bank, which has been designated by the U.N. and the United States for its role in facilitating the sales of conventional arms, ballistic missiles, and related items. The Treasury Department also targeted Leader (Hong Kong) International Trading Limited, a Hong Kong-based firm, for its links to the Korea Mining Development Trading Corporation, the DPRK's premier arms dealer and exporter of missile- and weapon-related goods.

We will continue to take national measures as appropriate. We are also working closely with the U.N. Security Council's DPRK sanctions committee and its Panel of Experts, the EU and like-minded partners, and others around the globe to harmonize our sanctions programs and to ensure the full and transparent implementation of UNSCRs 1718, 1874, and 2087, which remain the heart of the multilateral sanctions regime.

Sanctions are not a punitive measure, but rather a tool to impede the development of North Korea's nuclear and missile programs and proliferation-related exports, as well as to make clear the costs of North Korea's defiance of its international obligations. Working toward our endgame—the verifiable denuclearization of the Korean Peninsula in a peaceful manner—will require an openness to meaningful dialogue with the DPRK. But the real choice is up to Pyongyang.

We remain committed to authentic and credible negotiations to implement the September 2005 Joint Statement of the Six-Party Talks and to bring North Korea into compliance with its international obligations through irreversible steps leading to denuclearization. The President made this clear last November when he said, ". . . let go of your nuclear weapons and choose the path of peace and progress. If you do, you will find an extended hand from the United States of America." But let me state the obvious: North Korea's reckless provocations have certainly raised the bar for a return to dialogue.

The United States will not engage in talks for the sake of talks. Rather, what we want are negotiations that address the real issue of North Korea's nuclear program. Authentic and credible negotiations therefore require a serious, meaningful change in North Korea's priorities demonstrating that Pyongyang is prepared to meet its commitments and obligations to achieve the core goal of the September 2005 joint statement: the verifiable denuclearization of the Korean Peninsula in a peaceful manner.

This leads to some other important principles. First and foremost, the United States will not accept North Korea as a nuclear-armed state. We will not reward the DPRK for the absence of bad behavior. We will not compensate the DPRK merely for returning to dialogue. We have also made clear that U.S.-DPRK relations cannot fundamentally improve without sustained improvement in inter-Korean relations and human rights. Nor will we tolerate North Korea provoking its neighbors. These positions will not change.

In the meantime, active U.S. diplomacy on North Korea—on a wide range of issues—continues. Close coordination with our valued treaty allies, the ROK and Japan, remains central to our approach.

ROK President Park Geun-hye and President Obama agree on the need for continued close U.S.-ROK coordination on a range of security issues, including North Korea. We are confident of President Park's commitment to the U.S.-ROK alliance and anticipate close consultation with her administration on its North Korea strategy. Close consultation will also continue with Japan. During his visit to Washington in late February, Japanese Prime Minister Shinzo Abe and President Obama agreed to continue working together closely in responding to the threat posed by North Korea, including through coordination on sanctions measures.

We have also expanded our engagement by developing new dialogues on North Korea with key global actors who have joined the rising chorus of regional and global voices calling on North Korea to fulfill its commitments, comply with its international obligations, and refrain from provocative acts that undermine regional security and the global nonproliferation regime.

China, however, remains central to altering North Korea's cost calculus. Both geography and history have endowed the People's Republic of China with a unique—if increasingly challenging—diplomatic, economic, and military relationship with the DPRK. Close U.S.-China consultations on North Korea will remain a key locus of our diplomatic efforts in the weeks and months ahead as we seek to bring further pressure to bear on North Korea and, over the longer term, seek genuine diplomatic openings to push forward on denuclearization.

While denuclearization remains an essential focus of U.S. policy, so, too, does the welfare of North Korea's nearly 25 million people, the vast majority of whom bear the brunt of their government's decision to perpetuate an unsustainable, self-impoverishing military-first policy. While the DPRK devotes limited resources to developing nuclear weapons and ballistic missiles and devising ways to avoid sanctions, one in three North Korean children is chronically malnourished, according to a 2009 UNICEF estimate. An elaborate network of political prison camps in the country is reportedly estimated to contain 100,000–200,000 inmates, who are subjected to forced labor, torture, and starvation. It has been reported that whole families have been condemned—in most cases without trial—when one member commits an alleged crime. The courageous and charismatic Shin Dong-hyuk, whose life story is chronicled in Blaine Harden's excellent book, "Escape from Camp 14", was born in one of the most infamous political prison camps and spent the first 23 years of his life there. He was not only tortured and subjected to forced labor, but was also cruelly made to witness—at the age of 14—the execution of his mother and his brother.

Even outside this prison-camp system, the North Korean Government dictates nearly all aspects of people's lives through a highly structured social classification system called songbun, which it uses to divide North Korea's population into categories. This system, in turn, determines access to education and health care, employment opportunities, place of residence, and marriage prospects. Improving human rights conditions is an integral part of our North Korea policy, and how the DPRK addresses human rights will have a significant impact on prospects for improved U.S.-DPRK ties.

The world is increasingly taking note of the grave, widespread, and systematic human rights violations in the DPRK and demanding action. U.N. High Commissioner for Human Rights Navi Pillay has called for an in-depth international inquiry to document abuses. We support this call, and next week, my colleague Special Envoy for North Korean Human Rights Issues Robert King will travel to Geneva to attend the U.N. Human Rights Council's 22nd session, where he will call attention to North Korea's human rights record and urge the adoption of an enhanced mechanism of inquiry into the regime's abuses against the North Korean people.

We continue, meanwhile, to engage countries across the globe to raise awareness about North Korea and enlist their help in pushing for action. We are also working with international and nongovernmental organizations to improve the situation on the ground for the North Korean people, including by supporting the flow of independent information into the DPRK. Working with the Broadcasting Board of Governors, Voice of America, Radio Free Asia, and independent broadcasters in the ROK, we aim to provide information to the North Korean people and—over the longer term—plant the seeds for the development of civil society.

The Obama administration's dual-track policy of engagement and pressure toward the DPRK reflects a bipartisan recognition that only a policy of openness to dialogue when possible, combined with sustained, robust pressure through sanctions when necessary, can maximize prospects for progress in denuclearizing North Korea.

Progress on this decades-old problem will not be achieved easily or quickly. We cannot and should not dignify or, worse, feed the North Korean narrative that U.S. actions determine DPRK behavior. North Korea makes its own choices, selects its own timing, and is alone responsible for its actions. Similarly, we need to bear in mind that this is certainly not now—if it ever truly was—solely or even primarily a bilateral U.S.-DPRK issue. It is, rather, increasingly a global issue that requires an entrepreneurial approach, multilateral diplomacy and—yes—continuing, robust American leadership.

But above all else, genuine progress requires a fundamental shift in North Korea's strategic calculus. The DPRK leadership must choose between provocation or peace, isolation, or integration. North Korea will not achieve security, economic prosperity, and integration into the international community while it pursues nuclear weapons, threatens its neighbors, tramples on international norms, abuses its own people, and refuses to fulfill its longstanding obligations and commitments.

The international community has been increasingly clear about this, and so have we. The DPRK leadership in Pyongyang faces sharp choices. And we are working to further sharpen those choices. If the North Korean regime is at all wise, it will reembark on the path to denuclearization for the benefit of the North Korean people, the northeast Asia region, and the world.

Thank you again for the opportunity to appear before you today. I am happy to answer any questions you may have.

The CHAIRMAN. Thank you, Ambassador.

We will start a round and I will start.

Let me just take off of that almost closing comment that you made, that real progress depends upon North Korea changing its strategic calculus. The question is, What is it that we and our allies can do to affect changing North Korea's strategic calculus so that it moves in a different direction? And in that context, isn't really the key here, despite everything else that we are in the midst of pursuing, China and its potential influence with the North Koreans? And if that is the case, how is it that we can get the Chinese to be more robust in their efforts to get North Korea to change its strategic calculus?

Ambassador DAVIES. Yes. Well, you have asked probably the biggest question that can be asked about North Korea policy, and I think you are hitting on key themes here.

Changing North Korea's calculus is proving to be a challenge. Administrations of both stripes have been at this at least since Ronald Reagan was President and one can argue even before that.

What we are attempting to do is continue to present a united front in terms of, if you will, concentric circles beginning with our allies in the region, extending out to our partners in the six-party process, China and Russia, and then, going beyond that, to try to build an international coalition that understands the threat that North Korea poses to the international system, not just on nonproliferation, but on human rights, how it comports itself in the international financial system, and so forth. North Korea appears not yet to be absorbing those lessons, but we will continue to certainly sharpen them working with our colleagues and with our friends.

At a more basic level, we are working very closely, as we have for decades, with our South Korean ally to ensure that should North Korea miscalculate—and we call on them not to do that once again in the face of these new threats emerging from Pyongyang even in recent hours and days. We work with the South Koreans to make sure that we are ready from an alliance standpoint militarily to deal with any threats that arise. So that is very much at the macrolevel, if you will, how we are dealing with this problem.

You mentioned China. You are absolutely right about China. China is a critical piece of this challenge. They are North Korea's closest neighbor. They are often North Korea's protector. They are certainly an ally of North Korea. They have had a special relationship of sorts for quite a while. So we are concentrating a lot of diplomatic energy and effort on deepening our dialogue with China to present to them the proposition that there is still a peaceful, diplomatic way forward to deal with the North Korea issue. However, it will not work and cannot work unless China steps up, plays its full role in bringing home to Pyongyang the choices it faces and setting the table, if you will, for any return to negotiations.

I am afraid that the history of trying to draw North Korea into talks that can deal with its nuclear program, its missile program, and all of the other issues that we are concerned about has not been a fully successful one because the North Koreans have often been able to split us.

We think it is time to work more closely with China but also, of course, with our close allies and other partners in the six-party process to bring home to North Korea the choices it faces and to try to direct them——

The CHAIRMAN. Let me pursue that with you. For China, it seems to me—and correct me if I am wrong—there are two calculus here. One is they can do what they are doing with us at the United Nations today, which is pursue a set of new sanctions, and that will rattle the North Koreans to some extent. Or they can choose to go ahead and significantly cut back on that which is essential to North Korea's existence which is its assistance directly in fuel, as well as other sources. That would be far more significant.

From your perspective, what is the Chinese calculus then? Now they are joining us—we welcome that—at the Security Council. But they have a much bigger, more significant ability by virtue of the incredible assistance it gives North Korea.

Ambassador DAVIES. Sure. I think the safest thing to say about the Chinese calculus is it is evolving. I mean, yesterday we were greeted with the news, somewhat stunningly, that Chairman Mao's grandson, who was a general in the Peoples Liberation Army, called on North Korea to move forward on denuclearization. So there are some stunning developments occurring within China. One could almost describe it as the beginnings of a debate about how China will deal with its neighbor. Relations have not always gone smoothly of late between the two countries.

Now, I do not think it is up to us to try to figure out how to engage too deeply in that internal dialogue in China, but I think those are very helpful signs.

You are right. China is always the "get out of jail free" card for North Korea. They can always provide ways for the North Koreans to export materials, import materials, should they wish.

China, however, is part of the Security Council. I have just been given a note that the resolution has passed. The Chinese played a big role in crafting that resolution. It contains lots of new provisions that we could talk about.

So I think that there are signs that China is beginning to step up even more robustly to play its role. They say that they enforce these sanctions. We take them at their word. We trust but verify on that front and will continue to engage the Chinese to deepen our dialogue and to ensure that the Chinese do the maximum amount they can to deal with this problem.

The CHAIRMAN. Senator Corker.

14

Senator CORKER. Thank you, Mr. Chairman.

Again, Ambassador, thank you for your testimony.

I hear of the things that you are working on and we thank you for your work. And we understand this has been going on for 20 years and through many administrations. But when you talk about verifiable denuclearization, it seems to me that we continue to go in the opposite direction. And while we are talking today, I know, at the Security Council about some additional sanctions, it feels to me more like we are at a real crossroads, that this is not about additional sanctions, but we are at a crossroads where if something does not happen soon, there is no way that we can begin talking about verifiable denuclearization.

Do you agree with that, or do you think, just adding on additional pressures in the way we have been doing it, will work at some point?

Ambassador DAVIES. Well, I think it has to be a combination of all of the above plus more. I mean, I think we need to continue to press North Korea when necessary, and right now it is necessary to do that because they are in a provocation's phase. And so, therefore, you are getting the reaction from the U.N. Security Council. So I think pressure through sanctions is important.

I also think we need to stay strong in our alliance with the ROK, present a united front there, continue to sharpen and deepen our capabilities.

I also think it is important to continue to build this international coalition. I mean, 80 nations is somewhat stunning. You have got nations like South Africa, Brazil, even Communist nations like Laos and Vietnam, issuing statements condemning this most recent nuclear test. So the Greek chorus out there in the world is growing in volume.

And you are right. That is only good as far as it goes because what is most important is to change North Korea's calculus. So, therefore, we need to also be ready to engage North Korea in credible and authentic talks, if we can ever see that they are prepared to take real steps to denuclearize and to address our concerns. I think all of those things are exceedingly important.

And I think also, very quickly, we need to take account of what we have achieved over the last 60 years. We have worked with South Korea and helped them create a bit of an economic miracle. I think the ratio is now 36 to 1 in terms of the amount of goods and services produced per capita by the average South Korean as against the average North Korean. So things are not going well from the standpoint of the correlation of forces when it comes to North Korea right now.

So I think we move on all these fronts diplomatically, militarily, in terms of the international coalition. I think we need to keep drawing attention to their human rights, and I think by continuing to press them and continuing to present to them the opportunity, should they choose to accept it, to come talk to the international community and find a different way forward, away from provocations, away from bluster, away from threats, and move toward a different future that is absolutely available for them, I am at least guardedly optimistic that at some point they will see that is the way to go. And I think that is why we need to stay true to our principles and keep that pressure on.

Senator CORKER. I know you talked about us ensuring that Japan and South Korea and our other allies understand that we are going to be there to protect them. And yet, I think you are aware that we are not investing in modernization here in our own country regarding our nuclear armament as we should. Does that create any concerns with our allies that they see us really falling behind and not doing the things in our own country to ensure that that deterrence is there?

Ambassador DAVIES. I mean, to be fair, I work for the State Department, and that is a question ultimately for our Defense Department and defense planners, but I can take a bit of a stab at it.

Senator CORKER. If you will, take a short stab.

Ambassador DAVIES. I will take a short stab.

I have not seen in my frequent travels in Japan and the ROK that there are really deep concerns that our commitment to them is at all in jeopardy, and I think because we have begun what is called popularly the "pivot to Asia," we have begun to devote even more resources to the Asian theater, and I think that has gone, to a great extent, to reassure them.

Senator CORKER. So, you know, the mechanism that is funding this nuclear activity uses illicit activities. And we have ways of countering that. There are some people that are saying we should call the entire North Korean Government as a money laundering concern, and we could then enforce against third-party entities, some of which might reside in China. Could you talk to us about ways of getting involved in that illicit activity or stopping it so that it is not funding what they are doing from a nuclear proliferation standpoint and what your thoughts are about us actually being involved in clamping down on entities that are allowing that money to flow through?

Ambassador DAVIES. Well, some of the sanctions that have been part of the now many resolutions that have been passed get at this. I think it is important that we remain vigilant.

Senator CORKER. But at present, they are not really doing what needs to be done. I realize that some of the sanctions get at that.

Ambassador DAVIES. Sure.

Senator CORKER. But we are still not stopping the flow of money to these nuclear activities from illicit concerns. And is there more that we should be doing there?

Ambassador DAVIES. Well, I think we are slowing it, and I think that that is good because it makes it more difficult for the North Koreans to gain the inputs they need for their WMD program. I think it is important, though, in a kind of a, you know, all-aspects policy to look at that. That is something we continue to work on.

It is interesting. I will be quick here. If you look at the trend over a period of years, there was a time not so many years ago when these problems with supernotes, with methamphetamine exports, with the counterfeiting of cigarettes and drugs—this was really epidemic. I am not saying it is not still a problem. It is and we are very vigilant about it. But a lot of the steps that were taken by the international community led by the United States, I think, did a good job of making it much more difficult for them to do that. A lot more work to do. No question about it. I think you are right. It ought to be a focus of attention.

Senator CORKER. I know my time is up. I want to say I do agree with efforts to point out the human rights issues that are taking place. I think that helps us build an even greater coalition. And I would love to hear at some point about how we might influence the citizens there through a better broadcast activity taking place there.

But thank you for your testimony and I look forward to the rest of your answers.

Ambassador DAVIES. Thank you, sir.

The CHAIRMAN. Senator Udall.

Senator UDALL. Thank you, Chairman Menendez.

Thank you, Ambassador, for being here. I very much appreciate your service and willingness to go into these difficult situations.

Could you tell us with regard to the WMD programs, what is the current estimate of when North Korea would have a warhead-missile combination that could strike the United States? And what are the most effective means to prevent this from occurring or slowing down progress in that area?

Ambassador DAVIES. A great question and it is a subject of a lot of debate among some highly qualified experts in the government and then among the expert community beyond, people like Dr. Sig Hecker out at Stanford who have tremendous expertise here.

Senator UDALL. He was the director of our national laboratory at Los Alamos.

Ambassador DAVIES. Absolutely. Yes, he is a good friend. He is a national treasure. That is exactly right.

What I am going to have to do is take a dive on this one, sir, because you are asking a question that really does go deeply into intelligence matters. I love the lights of cameras, but I think with all that attention, I would really rather not get into what I know. And I have to be honest that I am not an expert on these matters.

So I think, though, as a general proposition, a lot of what is written in the popular literature about this by the think tanks and others is not too far off in terms of the estimates, some of which you have alluded to.

But I am sorry. I cannot get into those highly classified intelligence matters.

Senator UDALL. I understand that, but I wanted you to just give us a general answer as you did. I think various folks have talked about a matter of months or even a year or so in those kinds of situations. And I am sure that we will be getting briefings on that.

You know, a lot has been said about China's great cyber wall which blocks information critical of the Communist Party or policies from the Chinese people. But my understanding is North Korea has even a more robust restrictive policy in terms of the Internet. And it seems to me that one of the things we are seeing around the world, when you see democracy movements, is the Internet playing a role, the people being connected, people turning out in the streets as a result of that interconnectedness. And you may have noticed recently—and I know the administration did not bless this, but our former Governor, Governor Richardson, and

Google's Eric Schmidt recently visited to try to, I think, promote the idea of the Internet in North Korea.

And I was wondering should the United States be actively engaged in helping to create access to the Internet in North Korea? And do you believe that this is in the interest of the North Korean people as well as other countries in the region?

Ambassador DAVIES. Yes, a great question. And that is right. It is in our interests to do that, but it is a tough target set to convince the North Koreans to open up. While we were not crazy about the timing of the Richardson-Schmidt trip to Pyongyang, I was pleased to see Eric Schmidt make those statements. I think that was a very important challenge that he kind of laid down to the North Koreans.

Funny things are happening in North Korea. Interesting things are happening in North Korea that could eventually have an effect. You have 1.5 million cell phones now mostly among the elite and on a closed system, so huge limits there. They are not able to access the outside. But nonetheless, it promotes the spread of information within North Korea.

We know from lots of good studies that have been done by private organizations interviewing these 23,000 North Korean refugees who found their way to South Korea, that there is a surprising degree of understanding and knowledge in North Korea about the world outside their borders. South Korean soap operas are popular, and it probably is a bit of a shock to North Koreans when they get a thumb drive and they stick it in their machine and they watch one of these to see South Koreans with one and two cars in their garages and flat screen TVs and all the rest. So I think that the media picture in North Korea is changing. That is important. That is happening organically because of the trade between China and North Korea.

And I think we do need to look at entrepreneurial ways to promote more of that, get more information in. I think broadcasting is a big part of that. The Broadcasting Board of Governors spends a lot of time on this issue. We work with the ROK on that as well. We work with private groups. There are a number of NGOs, a number of evangelical organizations, and others who work hard to try to alleviate the challenges faced by average North Koreans, and their presence in the country I think is a great way to bring to the North Koreans an image of what Americans and the outside world are like.

So I think across all of these fronts, there is much that is happening. There is much more to do. And I am very glad you raised it.

Senator UDALL. Ambassador, back to the nuclear weapons, and I think this one is much less in the classified area. Is getting North Korea to dismantle its nuclear weapons still the goal of U.S. policy, and under what conditions might North Korea give up its nuclear weapons?

Ambassador DAVIES. It is still the goal of United States policy to achieve a Korean Peninsula that is free of nuclear weapons. The United States a generation ago removed our few short-range weapons that we had there.

We know this is not going to happen overnight even if we are able to get some sort of a diplomatic process started. I was personally engaged in following up the tremendous work that Ambassador Steve Bosworth did before he left my position to try to draw out the North Koreans to begin a process where we could go down that road and get them to, first of all, bound their nuclear program and eventually give them up.

I think there is still a chance for diplomacy. There is still a chance for the six-party talks to work, but it will require a united front on the part of all of us who are part of it. And most of all, it will require a change of calculus in Pyongyang, and that is what we are working to. But I am hopeful we can get to that future. I am hopeful that within a generation or so we could see a very different picture on the peninsula, and that is what we are working toward.

Senator UDALL. Thank you, Ambassador.

Thank you, Mr. Chairman.

The CHAIRMAN. Thank you.

Senator Rubio.

Senator RUBIO. Thank you, Mr. Chairman.

Thank you for being here with us. I know this is a difficult assignment you have been given by evidence of the fact that Ambassador Rodman last week visited North Korea and was not able to accomplish much either.

Ambassador DAVIES. Yes, but he gave up the baseline. That was the problem.

Senator RUBIO. I know.

You said a moment ago that you are guardedly optimistic that at some point this could be resolved through negotiations. I want to share with you my impressions based on the work we have done here and in some other committees that I serve on and get your impressions of that.

My impressions are that the North Korean regime—what they seek more than anything else is legitimacy and acceptance for who they are and what they are. And in essence, what they are looking for is the following. They want the world to accept them as a nuclear power. They want to be legitimized as a government that the world accepts as is despite all of the atrocities they commit and all the weird things they do abroad. And they want to be accepted and they want to be insulated from foreign interference in their affairs. And they have concluded that the only way they can accomplish these things is by being a nuclear power. And their strategy for moving forward on all these things is this series of escalations with potential off-ramps along the way that they conduct.

So, for example, they do these tests on the missiles. They conduct weapons tests. They say outrageous things like they are going to—I forgot their exact rhetoric used a week ago about wiping out the U.S. forces if they conduct a joint exercise. I think it was last night or this morning that they said they were going to strike us here in the homeland.

The point is that they use this escalating rhetoric and the actions that they take to further all this and to scare people or to get a reaction from the world toward one goal, and that one goal is very simple, to get the world to say, fine, North Korean regime, you can keep your weapons. We will accept you as who you are. That is their goal.

And I am not sure how we can negotiate them out of that position at this point. I think that is very difficult. For example, I think they sit there and decide, do we want to be Muammar Qaddafi or Saddam Hussein or do we want to be here forever and be able to hold onto this thing. And once we have a nuclear weapon and particularly once we have the capability of striking the United States at the homeland, they will have no choice but to accept us. And everything they do between now and then is just to delay or buy time or to scare us into a position of negotiation.

That does not mean I do not also hope that one day they will wake up and say, hey, this is bad for us. I just do not think a government like this can survive if they had to somehow get rid of their weapons and engage the world in a civilized way. And that is my concern. Why does this matter? For two reasons. And this is what I really wanted to share with you.

No 1, because I believe that if you are Japan, if you are South Korea, if you are other countries in the region, if North Korea continues to expand and, in fact, it gets global acceptance of their nuclear program, they are going to want one as well. So I think this fear of an escalation of nuclear weapons in the region is very real.

And the second concern that we have is that other countries are measuring their behavior. I think Iran is closely watching what is happening with North Korea. By the way, Iran has very similar goals. They want to be accepted as the government that they are, and they want to be insulated from foreign interference. And they think the nuclear weapons system is the way to do it. And they are watching very closely the way North Korea is being treated by the global community and determining from that how they need to proceed forward.

So I do not share this guarded optimism. I hope I am wrong. I really do. But the reality of it is, I think, the best we can hope for here is three things.

No. 1, we have to do everything we can to delay and preferably prevent them from accomplishing the goal of being able to reach the United States or the West with these weapons.

No 2, we should never allow the world to forget who these people are and what they are doing. And their list of atrocities is too long to catalog here today, but they kidnap people abroad. Any religion, particularly Christianity, is banned, punishable by death. Google has begun to catalog all these gulags that they have all over the country. The list goes on and on.

And third, I think we need to begin to create the conditions, God willing, for reunification, which is impossible today. Today that is not going to happen. But we do not know when the moment comes if those conditions become possible. And I think we need to do everything we can, along with our partners in the region and the world, to create the conditions where hopefully one day we could have a unified, democratic, peaceful Korea. And that is not possible today, but we can begin to create the conditions where hopefully one day that will be possible. Who could have predicted East Germany would have fallen, but it did. And one of the best ways we can do that is to strengthen and continue to strengthen our relationship economically and militarily with South Korea.

Those are my general impressions of this issue. I know that as a diplomat, your job is to try to bring a resolution to this that is negotiated. I just do not think that is going to happen with this guy because I think they are convinced that the only way they are ever going to accomplish what they want is by having a nuclear program and being able to hold the world hostage with it.

Ambassador DAVIES. Thanks so much. And let me just quickly—I mean, I do not disagree with anything you have said. This is one of the hardest foreign policy problems out there and not just for this particular administration but for many predecessor administrations. So you are right about all that.

Everything you prescribe I think is being done in one form or another: delaying their acquisition of these materials, working hard—and here Ambassador Joseph I think will have more to say—to prevent them from proliferating these technologies, never letting people forget the nature of this regime and what it is they have done to their own people, what it is they are doing to the international system by remaining an outlier.

And you talk about creating conditions for unification.

I think here you are right. What we need to do is continue to support the Republic of Korea.

What the ROK has done over the last couple of generations is nothing short of a miracle in terms of the way it has pulled itself up by its bootstraps, created the 11th-largest economy in the world, become a much, much more stronger nation. And I think we need to do all of this, and we certainly need to work more closely every day with the ROK and its new President, President Park Geunhye, to present this united front to North Korea and to do that also more broadly.

Within hours of their nuclear test, all of the other five parties, China and Russia included, issued statements denouncing what they had done.

So I agree with you.

Senator RUBIO. Can I just ask about the: Are we potentially in the midst of a recalibration among Chinese policymakers with regard to the utility of their current situation with North Korea? Is it possible that we are in the moment that the Chinese are looking at the situation and saying they are no longer what they once were? We really do not need the headache that these guys are.

Ambassador DAVIES. Well, you know, we might be. They are clearly not pleased in Beijing that every time they have tried to impress upon the North Koreans that they should take a different path, North Korea thumbs their nose at them. And we have seen stunning developments, articles appearing in the press that have to have been done with the knowledge of the central authorities. I mentioned Chairman Mao's grandson speaking out on this issue. You have got the Chinese blogosphere and netizens in China who, after Fukushima Daiichi, are saying what goes here. There is a nuclear test right across the border with North Korea. This country is still testing nuclear weapons 15 years after the last country tested a weapon. So things are changing in China.

What does it all mean? Where is it all headed? Will it create a fundamental shift in their strategic calculus? Very, very hard to say, but we are watching it closely.

The CHAIRMAN. Senator Cardin.

Senator CARDIN. Thank you very much, Mr. Chairman, and thank you for your testimony.

There are three major challenges that I want to talk about. You have already talked about them.

One, it is clear that North Korea is moving aggressively on its nuclear weapons program.

Second, as Senator Rubio pointed out, the record on human rights violations in the country is one of the worst of any country in the world, the way they treat their people, no opportunity for dissent, no opportunity for criticisms. Their kidnapping and torture are notorious.

And the third is the condition of their own people, the level of poverty, the level of hunger.

So I want to ask you three points that have been raised.

One is that North Korea has threatened to cut off the military hotline. How important is that in dealing with the threat of confrontation?

Second, the United Nations is looking at a commission on human rights. Should we have any confidence that that, in fact, would put an adequate spotlight on what is happening?

And the third is our contact in North Korea is limited. We do not have a great deal of NGOs to work with. We are not providing any significant aid at all. Should we be reevaluating the United States participation with NGOs to try to reach out to deal with the population itself in North Korea?

Ambassador DAVIES. Great questions. Let me be quick about that.

The hotline cutoff. They have done this before. It is one of the things they do on occasion. I do not know that it is necessarily the case that this latest threat to cut off the hotline—or perhaps they have already cut the line—is going to be, at the end of the day, much different from what we have seen in the past. Nonetheless, it is serious.

Senator CARDIN. Have we used it in the past?

Ambassador DAVIES. Yes. At the Peace Village on the border, it has often been used to convey messages back and forth.

Your question about what is happening in Geneva and the likely, we hope, establishment for the first time of a permanent mechanism, a commission of inquiry, to look at North Korean human rights, I think this is a significant development. It is somewhat stunning that this has not been the case in the past. But anyway, the United Nations is, we hope, going to take that step. And I think that it is not a magic bullet, but I think it will be a great way for the entire international community institutionally and indefinitely to look at what is going on in North Korea and to broadcast to the rest of the world the results of their efforts.

On NGOs——

Senator CARDIN. Before we leave that point, are there still hurdles that have to be overcome for that commission to be established?

Ambassador DAVIES. Well, it is not done yet. The Human Rights Council has not looked at it. And having served a couple of years in Vienna working in the U.N. system, I know nothing is done until it is done in U.N.-land. So we will see.

But we have reason to believe that there is the right kind of correlation of forces. The European Union is behind this. Japan is behind it. The ROK has just announced their support for this mechanism. We are actively seeking it. And of course, I had mentioned in my statement that U.N. officials are behind it and promoting it. So I think the planets are lining up. It is going to happen, I hope. And we are going to do what we can to make it happen. And it will have an effect.

On NGOs, that is a great point. Yesterday during the snow day that wasn't, I was in the office and I was on a wonderful conference call with about seven NGOs, Mercy Corps, GRS, many of them religiously based. These people do heroic work in North Korea. And it is very unsung. They get in there. They do medical programs. They get out of Pyongyang, that walled city where the elite lives, and they get into the countryside and they do everything from tuberculosis work to digging wells to helping hospitals and dental clinics. You name it. And I think it is important that we do everything we can to kind of clear the path for them to do what they can do. It is not easy. And one of the concerns they had was about sanctions and whether sanctions will affect their ability to bring things into North Korea to do the work they have got to do.

I think we need to try to find a way—and there is a bit of a carve-out in the language of the resolution—to promote their work because I think that is exceedingly important that this kind of people-to-people work go forward. Why? Because one-third of North Koreans, according to a number of studies, are severely, chronically malnourished. They are clearly forgotten by the elites who live in Pyongyang building amusement parks and holding rock concerts and so forth. And so it is very, very important that we do what we can to work with them.

Senator CARDIN. We have, in the past when we have imposed sanctions, tried to figure out ways that we can get direct aid to NGOs that we have confidence in to provide the type of humanitarian aid that is appropriate. Do we have confidence that if that aid were to be made available, that the NGO network is strong enough and there is enough accountability that we would be able to assure that the aid, in fact, went for the designated purpose and was not diverted to compromise the importance of the sanctions?

Ambassador DAVIES. Well, the NGOs take it very seriously. They have got decades of experience. They are very good about it. A lot of their work is scaled such that it is a lot less likely that the regime is going to try to divert the resources that they provide, the services to the military or the elites. I have been impressed as I have looked at the specifics of these programs that they have underway. They have, to a great extent, figured out how to do this, and whether it is flood relief or whether it is bringing nutritional supplements to malnourished children, they are one of the ways we ought to go. And when we have done big feeding programs in North Korea—there was the 500,000 metric ton program under the previous administration that the North Koreans cut off only about a third of the way into it. And this most recent one we tried to put in place—we do most of that work through U.S. NGOs because they are that good and they have the right understanding of how to ensure that the goods and services they provide get to the people who need them.

Senator CARDIN. I will just make a final point. For Congress to allow that type of assistance, we need to know and have confidence that we can account for how the aid is being used since we are not present in the country to be able to do that. We have to have that type of confidence. So it is something that you need to be able to build up as far as the questions that will be asked in Congress.

Ambassador DAVIES. Absolutely. Thank you, sir.

The CHAIRMAN. Senator Johnson.

Senator JOHNSON. Thank you, Mr. Chairman.

Mr. Davies, welcome. Thank you for your testimony.

Can you just kind of bring me up to speed in terms of the progress of the new leader in terms of his consolidation of power and how much of that consolidation really leads to the high jinx we have been seeing here recently?

Ambassador DAVIES. Well, that is a really hard target. A lot of terrific intelligence professionals work at that. We stay in close touch with our European allies, some of whom have small embassies there. I just, a week ago, spent a couple of hours with the ambassador of one of those nations who had lots of insights to provide about the thinking of the government.

Just as a general matter, I think what has happened was, you know, Kim Jong-un came into power the beginning of last year on the death of his father in mid-December in 2011. There was then this period that lasted a few months where everybody was saying, oh, this may be a new day. He is a young Gorbachev. One think tanker even talked about a Camelot moment occurring in North Korea. I personally was not buying any of this stuff at the time, nor were many in Government. But what we have seen is that that debate has gone away, that the hope for the kind of a more enlightened approach to these issues—that is fading fast.

I think he has consolidated his power. He has now got the six key titles. He is the head of the army, head of the military, head of the government. And remember, the logic of their system is such—it is such a strictly hierarchical, dictatorial, top-down system that in order for that system to operate as it has for the last three generations, there has to be a man at the top to whom all issues are referred and from whom all wisdom flows. So we think that he is, for all intents and purposes, in charge.

And as to why he has taken the steps he has taken, some of the purges, I think some of that has been consolidating his power, firing the generals and so forth, and then all of this tough talk going on—it is hard to say why they are doing that. I think a lot of it is just their classical reaction to the fact that the international community increasingly is coming together and making it tougher for them operate. So I think that is the kind of acting out that we often see from North Korea.

Senator JOHNSON. Thank you.

I am new to the committee, but I have certainly been watching the laying out of sanctions and then relaxing them a little bit, basically the dual strategy here. Can you tell me in your mind what was the most effective set of sanctions? I will start there. I mean, what worked best. But I also want you to speak to what mistakes were made. What lessons have we learned both in terms of the effectiveness of sanctions and how we maybe relaxed them and basically how the United States has been kind of played like Charlie Brown more than once here?

Ambassador DAVIES. Yes, but on sanctions I think what is important—the most important sanctions often tend to be the ones that have the buy-in of the broadest number of nations. And here I talked about the role of China and the importance of working with them to ensure that they follow through on their commitments when it comes to sanctions.

What is the most effective set of sanctions? That is hard to say. You know, I am tempted to say that probably the sanctions that have helped to cut off the flow of luxury goods is pretty important because it has prevented the regime, to some extent—they find ways around it, but of rewarding members of the elite.

But I think a more serious answer is that the sanctions that are getting at the nuclear program, getting at the missile program, preventing the inputs from going into North Korea that they need in order to build up those weapons of mass destruction programs, those are the most important.

This latest resolution that I was given a note that has passed in New York contains not only a tightening of the existing sanctions but it has got some new sanctions in it that get at that problem. And I think we need to keep building on that. I think what you will see is that there will then be national sanctions that will be promulgated by not just us but others in order to tighten sanctions down further.

But I think it is in the missile and nuclear areas where the sanctions are having the most effect and then finally, interdiction which is to say—and this new resolution has a lot of good stuff in it about preventing the export by North Korea of its armaments, which is a key source of income, by sea and by air. And there is a lot in this resolution that gets at that, and I think that is what we need to keep working on first and foremost.

Senator JOHNSON. Did we not freeze bank accounts at some point in time for the top leaders?

Ambassador DAVIES. We have done a number of financial sanctions that are more in this particular resolution approved just minutes ago. There are individual designations of key people and their apparatus who play key roles in exporting their materials, importing what they need to build up their programs, travel bans on these individuals, and so forth. So it is a combination of these individual designations, institutional designations, and then also the specific inputs, the actual machinery and technology that they need. And I think we just need to push on all of these fronts and keep it up.

Senator JOHNSON. Senator Rubio mentioned the word "recalibration," and somebody else talked about strategic calculus. Of the members of the six-party talks, what has been the most significant movement or most significant recalibration of the strategic calculus whether it is Russia, China, Japan? Can you just speak to that?

I mean, where has there been some movement just to give me some sense of that history?

Ambassador DAVIES. Well, I think the movement—it is a little bit like, I have to admit, watching paint dry sometimes. It is such a long process. But I think the movement has been incremental. I think the movement has been all of the various efforts, and there have been really quite a variety of approaches to this problem by various administrations in the past whether engagement, whether pressure, different architectures internationally, six-party talks. There were four-party talks at one point, and here Ambassador Bosworth can speak to a great deal of this. I think the biggest change has been just the steady accumulation of experience, of pressure, of sanctions over the years, over the decades, and I think that has made a huge difference.

And then the final thing I will say is that, you know, the world is beginning to wake up to a greater extent to this problem. It is still kind of stunning, as a diplomat, that 80 nations from every corner of the world would issue statements condemning North Korea's nuclear test. These are developments we would not have seen even a few years ago. So this coalition is building. It is growing. It is strengthening, and it is meaningful because these are people who send messages to North Korea. They send messages to China. And it is very difficult in an international system for a nation like North Korea to ignore the fact that increasingly their actions are seen as deleterious to the functioning of the world system and to the interests of these countries.

So it is hard for me to point to one particular recalibration that has occurred. Maybe what is going on in China will fit that bill. But I would just say that it is this incremental deepening and broadening of pressure on North Korea that has been most important.

Senator JOHNSON. OK, thank you.

The CHAIRMAN. Senator Murphy.

Senator MURPHY. Thank you very much, Mr. Chairman.

I wanted to start by talking about the North Korean economy. I think there is this sort of popular impression that the North Korean economy is sort of this vast wasteland of work camps and starving people, and while that is certainly true for a big part of the country, there is also a relatively stable economy in the capital. There is a class of ruling elites that are doing fairly well. And you mentioned in your response to Senator Johnson briefly about the impact that our sanctions have had on holding back luxury goods from that class of individuals that has seemingly been pretty resistant to the type of poverty that has struck the rest of the nation.

Can you talk a little bit about the state of the North Korean economy today? Can you talk a little bit about our relative success or lack of success in trying to change the calculus for the ruling elite based on their economic status and any new tools that may be at our disposal to try to change that?

Ambassador DAVIES. Yes. Well, the economy question is a great one, and there are a number of experts who look at this hard. It is tough to measure. They do not produce statistics that are at all reliable to indicate the scope of it.

Many people are fooled when they go to Pyongyang which, as I have said, is a bit of a walled city state. You cannot easily get in and get out where the elites live, and they see people with cell phones and they see a few more cars on the street, a few more restaurants, and they conclude that North Korea is really coming up in the world economically. I do not think that is the case.

They have some goods and services to offer to the world. They have mineral deposits that are of value certainly to China which seeks to exploit them and others. They export laborers to Russia and China and other places around the world who remit moneys to North Korea. Their economy in some sectors has done reasonably well.

But the problem, of course, is that their agriculture sector remains unreformed; their light industrial sector, the same. When the new leader came in, he made a number of promises about—hinted at reforms that he would institute. We have yet to see that. For whatever reason, he seems to have drawn back from going forward with those reforms. To some extent, reform of the North Korean economy would be good for the North Korean people, and the Chinese are often telling us that we should help the North Koreans reform their economy and we beg to differ on that.

And I am sorry. Your second question, sir?

Senator MURPHY. No. That was the first question.

The second one would be this. So to what extent is food aid an actual tool to recalibrate their strategic interests? We have certainly had success in these temporary agreements by exchanging food aid for concessions on their nuclear program, but of course, as we saw with the Leap Day Agreement, it can blow up within months.

Ambassador DAVIES. Sure.

Senator MURPHY. Is this a real pressure point in negotiations, or have they just used this as a means to sort of delay and delay and postpone?

Ambassador DAVIES. Yes. I think the latter is the case.

We do not link food assistance to political matters. What I found, when I came into the process toward the end of our yearlong effort to negotiate this deal with the North Koreans, was that the North Koreans were insisting that the offer we had made of 240,000 metric tons be linked to the concessions they were going to make on nuclear and missiles. So they enforced that linkage from their side. We do not use food as a weapon or a tool and we do not link it to political matters.

And no country has been more generous than the United States over the years in providing food to the North Korean people I think since 1989, if I have the statistic right or 1997. It has been on the order of some $800 million of food, almost 2 million metric tons. So we support the people of North Korea. We try—and it is not easy—to bring them aid and comfort, bring them food because it is quite clear that the authorities in Pyongyang do not care about what happens in the hinterland of North Korea, and they allow this malnutrition and sometimes, as was the case in the 1990s, starvation to occur.

So we do not link the two. I would never posit or put forward that food aid is something we should use as an inducement to political change or change on denuclearization.

Senator MURPHY. Thank you.

And then one last question on China, and you may have responded to this in response to Senator Menendez. But in particular to what Senator Rubio talked about with regard to the arms race that could develop in the region should they get full nuclear capacity, what does China think about that? I can understand that they could say, listen, we can control the North Koreans if we continue to be responsible for 70 percent of their economy. Even if they do get nuclear capacity, we can deal with that. But they have to understand that the balance of power in the region dramatically shifts if all of a sudden 10 years from now or 15 years from now there are three or four or five nuclear powers in the region. Is that a bright line for them? Do they view that as a serious threat?

Ambassador DAVIES. Well, I mean, the last thing I will do is speak for the Chinese on this. But there are signs that the Chinese are watching closely these debates that are occurring, in particular in Japan and the ROK among some. I do not think any consensus is developing or will develop in favor of going forward with developing nuclear weapons. I certainly hope not because it is important from the standpoint of the integrity of the Nonproliferation Treaty that they not go forward in doing that. But the Chinese are taking notice and I think it concerns them.

You know, one of the things that we say to them when we have these conversations about what is happening in North Korea is if you have concerns about America's kind of recalibration of its force posture toward Asia, then if North Korea continues to go in the same direction and we cannot find a way to work together to resolve it, you will see more of the same and you are not going to like it. You will see more developments such as the extension by the ROK of the range of its missiles. You will see more developments like the placement of TPY–2 radars in Japan. You will see more on missile defense. You will see more on the rest of it.

And so you have some voices in China talking about, oh, well, this is the United States trying to encircle us. It is not what we are trying to do at all. What we are trying to do is defend ourselves. And I think that they know these phenomena are related. And I think that they are concerned about it and we hope it becomes an incentive for China to step up and do a bit more, given their special relationship with North Korea, to try to resolve this problem. And we stand ready to work with the Chinese to do that.

The CHAIRMAN. Senator Kaine.

Senator KAINE. Thank you, Mr. Chairman.

Special Representative Davies, I am just going to pick up on the chairman's opening question, which I think we are all kind of grappling with. What is the right way to change the calculus with North Korea vis-a-vis the nuclear program? And many of the questions thus far have been about external measures, and I want to get to those in a second.

But I would like to get your sense on internal measures. You know, looking at the history of nations that have decided to abandon nuclear programs, often it has been an internal political calculus that has caused them to do so.

In looking at some of the events of the Arab Spring, you know, what struck me was that people grow to tolerate all over the world sadly and live under dictatorships, but they start to get restive under hereditary dictatorships. And so whether it was in Egypt in a time of potential transition to a new Mubarak or a Libya in a time of potential transition to a younger Qaddafi or Syria with a second Assad, once the dictatorship starts to become a hereditary dictatorship, then there is some restive possibility that a population decides that it wants to throw it off.

Let us talk about the internal dynamics of North Korea and just educate me a bit on that. I mean, is there any potential for internal dissent that could drive a rethinking of the nuclear program? And is there anything we can appropriately do? It is kind of like hydrofracking, you know, finding the microfissures and then doing things you can to widen them. Is there anything we can appropriately do to drive that dissent and increase it?

Ambassador DAVIES. We do not see signs of significant internal dissent in North Korea, and maybe that is often the case before changes occur. I do not know. So that presents a challenge to us to figure out where do you drill and what do you pump into that hole in order to engage in this kind of fracking. I love that image. So it is tough.

I think the important thing is to keep firing on all cylinders, to keep broadcasting into North Korea, to continue to work with our allies who do a great deal of this work with NGOs. I do think the situation is changing in North Korea. They are educated. They are, I think many of them, hungry for information about what is happening on the outside.

But when it comes to the classical stuff that we all know from history about, well, is there a unity army or is there somebody in the regime who is susceptible, there is nothing like that that presents itself to us right today that we can exploit or reach out to. And it makes it a very, very, very tough problem set.

Senator KAINE. And just explain that as somebody who is an expert in this area, the absence of this kind of visible dissent. And you are in good touch with nations that have diplomatic presence in North Korea. Is it just the sheer demoralization and poverty of those who do not have any credible ability to match up against a military power? Is it the long-term effects of famine? Is it a cultural—I mean, how would you describe what we are seeing elsewhere we do not see there, given famine, given the poor economic conditions that would drive dissent elsewhere?

Ambassador DAVIES. That is really hard for me to answer. I am not a lifelong North Korea expert.

I do not think we are going to know if and when that opportunity necessarily presents itself any better than we have in recent years when we have seen dramatic change in parts of the world where there were authoritarian or dictatorial systems. And the problem with North Korea is it is just the most hermetically sealed, highwalled, paranoid state out there. I do not think it really has its modern equivalent anywhere else in the world.

Senator KAINE. Since Albania fell——

Ambassador DAVIES. Maybe Albania.

Senator KAINE [continuing]. It does not have an equivalent.

Ambassador DAVIES. Maybe Albania.

So I have to admit that even though a lot of very dedicated, qualified people work this issue in the intelligence community, in our military, out of the State Department, and we do that on a daily basis, there is not anything there that I can point to right now as the pressure point, the fissure that we can exploit.

I keep coming back to the necessity for staying true to our principles, staying close to our allies, working hard with our partners, in particular China given their relationship, highlighting the human rights depredations in North Korea. And I believe that there will come a day when things will likely change. I do not think that North Korea has forever to make the strategic choice to go in a different direction that will involve reaching out to the rest of the world and fulfilling its promises and going down the path of denuclearization. That is it. They have got an off-ramp. There is a way that we can work this peacefully, diplomatically that we presented to them time and time again, and they have chosen not to take us up on it. We will continue to do it, and some day, I am convinced, when the pounds per square inch of pressure builds up enough, they may see the light and decide, well, maybe we ought to take door No. 1. I hope that is true.

Senator KAINE. Let me ask about external pressure. Good questions have been asked already about the five parties to the six-party talks and China especially. But there are other nations that we have strong relationships with that aid and abet or at least have interactions with the North Korean Government that probably help them to gain or continue momentum on their illicit activity, nations like Egypt and Pakistan and the UAE that are not a direct part of those talks. But talk about our abilities to utilize those relationships and, either through the U.N. action today or other actions, get them to stop anything that would promote North Korea's forward momentum on nuclear proliferation.

Ambassador DAVIES. That is a great question. We work at it all the time. There have been some successes. I mean, you are familiar with the Burma example where the new government has made the strategic decision to go in a different direction and to change the nature of its relationship with North Korea. That is very important. That will still take some time to play out and work through. The same is true of many of these other sort of traditional customers or states that have dealt with North Korea. Since the al-Kibar reactor was taken care of in Syria, I think that is a relationship that is no longer what it was.

So the truth is we take it case by case. We work with these countries that still maintain an arms relationship with North Korea. I think this effort to expand the international coalition and consensus about North Korea is important because the moral hazard of dealing with North Korea becomes a more important factor, I think, for many of these countries. But I guess the short and honest answer is it is a case-by-case effort that we undertake and we are seeking to step it up. And this resolution passed today in New York I think is going to help us, to a great extent, to get at that problem.

Senator KAINE. Great. Thanks very much.

The CHAIRMAN. Senator Flake.

Senator FLAKE. I apologize. I had a couple other markups and hearings going on.

I just want to ask—and I am not sure how this has been asked or answered before, but do you believe that for the reductions on our part as a result of these treaties will do anything to persuade the North Koreans to move ahead with reductions or not moving ahead with what they are doing? How effective is what we do or how persuasive is that with their own actions, or is that completely independent?

Ambassador DAVIES. Well, here I can draw on my couple of years working at the International Atomic Energy Agency where in the wake of the President's Prague speech where he set out his vision for a world without nuclear weapons, I found, representing the United States in that body, a 150-nation body, that that had a tremendous effect on convincing a lot of the fence-sitters around the world that the United States was serious about trying to move forward because if you go back to Eisenhower's nuclear bargain, which he laid out in his Atoms for Peace speech, you know, it was quite clear. Those with nuclear weapons would seek over time to— you know the whole thing—get rid of them. Those without would pledge not to acquire them. And so for many, many, many countries in the world, the United States demonstrating that it is serious about keeping up its end of the nuclear bargain has a tremendous effect.

Now, when it comes to North Korea, I am not going to spin you and tell you that the North Koreans are going to pack up their nuclear weapons and put them in a pile and burn them up if we pass further arms control treaties with Russia and so forth. But what it does is it has a tremendous effect on all 189 nations who are signatories of the Nonproliferation Treaty, and it makes it easier for us and others who care a lot about this treaty to move that agenda forward, reduces North Korea's running room, makes it tougher for North Korea to continue to claim that they need these weapons in order to defend themselves. And so I think it is a vital aspect of winning over hearts and minds globally and eventually setting up a set of circumstances in which it is very, very difficult if not, one hopes, eventually impossible for them to continue to maintain as an international outlier this commitment to develop nuclear weapons.

The CHAIRMAN. Senator Corker has one additional question.

Senator CORKER. Just one brief question. You know, I listened to you and I know that you are working hard and many people have for many, many years. But I think you basically, in answering some of the questions, have acquiesced and said, look, you know, this is probably going to continue on and we do not see any real changes and more pressure will be applied.

I am just curious. We have a situation with Iran where there is a redline, and we have been pretty bellicose about the fact that we would use military action to keep them from having nuclear weapons. And yet, in Korea, equally nutty folks, human rights even worse—and it is bad in Iran too. But why is it that we have a policy in North Korea that is so different than what we have in Iran when you have equally bellicose and, I would say, regimes that certainly are rogue regimes? Why would we have such a differentiating policy?

Ambassador DAVIES. Well, I think actually the policy has more commonalities than differences. In both cases what we seek to do is, as I said earlier, in the case of North Korea, use pressure when we have to use pressure and seek to exploit engagement when it is possible to engage them.

I do not agree that there has been no change. I think that the pressure of the sanctions, the coalitions we have built, the work in six-party, a lot of the diplomatic efforts in which the gentlemen to my right who will testify next were intimately involved went a great distance to——

Senator CORKER. But they are certainly way past any kind of redline that we would accept in Iran. They are certainly way beyond anything that we as a country have stated publicly that we would accept in Iran. So it seems to me that we have two very different policies here. I am just curious why that is the case.

Ambassador DAVIES. Well, I think we have two very different historical situations that have developed, and I think it is because of the different set of circumstances in both. I am not an Iran expert. I worked the issue when I was in Vienna, but that was some time ago. So I can quickly get myself in trouble by trying to compare the Iran case to the North Korea case.

But as the North Korea case has developed, I think that there have been some successes. I think we have slowed their efforts to create these weapons. I think we have built this coalition that is going to continue to decrease their running room and their space within which they can operate. I have faith that if we stick with our principles that have been devised on a bipartisan basis over 20–30 years, that we will see the kinds of changes that we would like to see.

And I am sorry. It is true. You know, these are pernicious problems. This is the land of a lot of bad alternatives. And so I think the way you deal with it is you stick to your principles. You stick to your allies. You make modest progress here, sometimes dramatic progress there. Occasionally there are setbacks, but you keep at it. And I think American leadership on this issue is absolutely essential. I think it has borne a lot of fruit. Sadly it has not changed the strategic situation yet, but I have got every confidence that if we keep at it, if we keep together, we are going to see sooner or later—hope it is sooner—the kinds of changes we hope are needed.

And I want to reemphasize this one point. It is up to North Korea to understand that it has another path that it can take. It has a partner in the international community that will engage with North Korea, but it has got to be the one to make this decision, make this strategic choice, move toward abandoning nuclear weapons and missiles. And if they do, there can be a very different future on the Korean Peninsula and one that will be for the benefit of all the Korean people, North and South.

Senator CORKER. Thank you, Mr. Chairman.

I think that is a highly aspirational statement that does not seem to be very based on reality today, but I thank you for your optimism. And yet, I will go back to my original premise and certainly would like to understand that more fully.

Thank you.

The CHAIRMAN. Well, let me just make an observation. First of all, we are very aspirational here. [Laughter.]

Ambassador DAVIES. You have to be on North Korea.

The CHAIRMAN. But I think in part just an observation on Senator Corker's question which is that, obviously, one of the reasons we have so vigorously pursued a sanctions regime on Iran is because Iran is not where North Korea is in terms of its nuclear program and we do not desire it to get to that point as North Korea has. So whether or not there was a different point in time in which maybe a previous administration should have adopted a very similar position as we have now with Iran, we are past that moment. And our question is how do we deal with the realities of the moment and try to change the dynamics, the strategic calculus both inside of North Korea and, I hope, the strategic calculus of China in this context, which plays a key role toward, hopefully, getting us to the point that we want to be.

With the thanks of the committee and for your staying power, we appreciate very much your appearing here, and we look forward to continuing dialogue with you and the administration on this critical issue.

As we excuse Ambassador Davies, let me call up our next panel.

Ambassador Stephen Bosworth who served for over a decade as dean of the Fletcher School of Law and Diplomacy at Tufts University, and from March 2009 to October 2011, served as the U.S. Special Representative for North Korea Policy. From 1997 to 2001, Ambassador Bosworth was the U.S. Ambassador to the Republic of Korea. From 1995 to 1997, he was the Executive Director of the Korean Peninsula Energy Development Organization, an intergovernmental organization established by the United States, the Republic of Korea, and Japan. And Ambassador Bosworth has a distinguished career in the U.S. Foreign Service for nearly three decades.

Please, gentlemen come on up and sit right at the table.

Joseph DeTrani is the president of the Intelligence and National Security Alliance. He previously worked as the Senior Advisor in the Office of the Director of National Intelligence, Director of ODNI's National Counterproliferation Center, and as the ODNI's North Korean Mission Manager. Prior to his work at ODNI, Ambassador DeTrani served at the Department of State as both a Special Envoy for Negotiations with North Korea and as the U.S. Representative to the Korea Energy Development Corporation. He has worked in numerous roles throughout the Central Intelligence Agency and has extensive experience in that regard as well.

Finally, Robert Joseph is the senior scholar at the National Institute for Public Policy. From 2005 to 2007, Ambassador Joseph was the Under Secretary of State for Arms Control and International Security, and from 2001 to 2004, he served in the National Security Council as Special Assistant to the President and the Senior Director for Proliferation Strategy, Counterproliferation and Homeland Defense. Ambassador Joseph also served in the Department of Defense as Principal Deputy Assistant Secretary of Defense for

International Security Policy and Deputy Assistant Secretary of Defense for Nuclear Forces and Arms Control.

So we have a very distinguished panel here.

I am going to ask each of you to summarize your statement in around 5 minutes. Your full statements will be entered into the record so we can have time for some dialogue here, as we move forward. We want to pick upon your expertise to draw some of the questions and answers to some of the issues that have already been raised with our previous panelist, Ambassador Davies.

And so we will start in the order that I recognized you: Ambassador Bosworth, Ambassador DeTrani, and Ambassador Joseph.

STATEMENT OF HON. STEPHEN W. BOSWORTH, DEAN, THE FLETCHER SCHOOL OF LAW AND DIPLOMACY, TUFTS UNIVERSITY, MEDFORD, MA

Ambassador BOSWORTH. Thank you very much, Mr. Chairman. I am grateful for the opportunity to appear before the committee.

I will not try to summarize the current scene with regard to North Korea. I think Ambassador Davies did that quite well. I would only say a few things as an opening.

First, this is obviously a very, very difficult problem, and it follows that there are no good options for dealing with it. If there were, I trust that some of us would have found those in the past.

Instead, I think what we have found is that North Korea, by and large, has continued to exceed reasonable expectations as to what they could accomplish technologically both in their missile program and in their nuclear program. Having followed this issue for now 20 years, I would venture to say that they have consistently outperformed the expectations of the outside world, and I do not think we have time to get into the question of why. But they have created a situation in which now they are demonstrably within reach over some period of time of being able to, as someone put it earlier today, mate a nuclear device with a missile, and that changes the strategic balance in a number of ways.

As I said, the options for dealing with them are very limited and very obscure. We can, as we have in the past at various times, simply stand back and wait for what we considered at the time to be the inevitable collapse. That policy has clearly not succeeded. We began waiting for their collapse back in the late 1980s, and when I last checked, they are still there.

Similarly, we can rely on a policy of containment and deterrence, which we will have to do in any event. But I think what we have found is that containment and deterrence do not prevent the threat from growing more acute.

Also, we can, of course—as has been hinted in various questions this morning—rely more heavily on China to somehow solve this problem for us. I am not optimistic that China is going to do that. I am encouraged by their apparent willingness to contemplate tougher sanctions as they have this last time around in the United Nations.

But I think China continues to face an essential conundrum which is that while on the one hand, they do not want North Korea to become a nuclear weapons state, on the other hand, they also do not want North Korea to collapse. And in their view, they are concerned that bringing sufficient pressure to bear on North Korea to stop their nuclear program, much less to dismantle it, would risk creating a situation in which North Korea could collapse. And for China, an equally undesirable outcome of all of this would be to wake up some morning and find that the border of South Korea is now the Yellow River because North Korea has collapsed and South Korea with a military alliance with the United States. That changes in a very fundamental way what has been called the correlation of forces on the Korean Peninsula. And Chinese strategic thinkers have to have this very much in mind.

All this being said, my own personal view is that at some point—I cannot say exactly when, but I would think sooner rather than later—we will come back to an effort to engage with North Korea in some manner only because the alternatives are so bleak. And I think that that probably is what we should try to do because we have no good options.

The question that will exist at that time is engage on what basis. Do we again seek to engage on the basis of denuclearization pretty much by itself at least as a primary objective, or do we seek to engage on a broader basis going back, for example, to the joint statement negotiated in the six-party process back in September 2005 in which all of the parties signed on to a four-goal/four-objective formulation: denuclearization, a peace treaty to replace the armistice of 1953, establishment of diplomatic relations among all parties concerned, and agreement to provide energy and economic assistance to North Korea.

In my view, it would be more productive to seek from the outset to engage with North Korea on the basis of that broader agenda which seeks, in my judgment, to get at what is really the fundamental problem on the Korean Peninsula, the problem which gives rise to the nuclear threat and that is the inherent weakness of North Korea and the strong conviction of the North Korean regime that it will not do anything which risks its demise.

So in my judgment, only by addressing these broader considerations of a peace treaty to replace the armistice, economic and energy assistance, and diplomatic relations do we have a prospect of getting at what remains and will remain our central and abiding concern which is the North Korean nuclear problem. But I think rather than simply focusing on that and trying to identify it and to try to resolve it in and of itself, which has not proven to be very feasible over the last several years, I think we would be much better off looking for a broader focus. And I think that the prior agreement of September 2005 provides the seed for such a broader agreement.

And with that, Mr. Chairman, I will conclude my remarks.

The CHAIRMAN. Thank you very much.

Ambassador DeTrani.

STATEMENT OF HON. JOSEPH DeTRANI, PRESIDENT, INTELLIGENCE AND NATIONAL SECURITY ALLIANCE, ARLINGTON, VA

Ambassador DeTRANI. Mr. Chairman, Senator Corker, members, thank you for the invitation.

My statement is on the record. Let me just offer a few comments.

I certainly agree with Ambassador Bosworth. Denuclearization is the name of the game with North Korea. Permitting North Korea to sustain their program, maintain that program and, as we see it, enhance their program with additional nuclear weapons, not only through plutonium but through uranium, would be a destabilizing factor for the region. Other countries will be looking to acquire similar capabilities—Senator Rubio asked that question, and I think it is a fair question. We are talking about the potential for a nuclear arms race. We are also talking about the potential for nuclear terrorism, and others who want to get their hands on nuclear materiels and nuclear devices.

In 2002, we confronted the North Koreans with their uranium enrichment program. It was a clandestine uranium enrichment program. They denied having that program. In 2010, they admitted to the program. The same gentleman who was mentioned this morning, Dr. Sig Hecker, was introduced to a facility at Yongbyon where they had 2,000, they said, functioning and operating centrifuges. As Dr. Hecker said at that time, this was a state-of-the-art facility. The assessment here is that North Korea was, and is, pursuing a uranium enrichment program to complement their plutonium program, all for nuclear weapons purposes. That is point one.

Point two—and I agree totally with Ambassador Bosworth—the September 2005 joint statement is a seminal statement. It speaks to a commitment that Kim Jong-il, Kim Jong-un's father, committed to where he said even in Beijing he commits to denuclearization. And that 2005 joint statement says very clearly that in exchange for economic assistance, security assurances, ultimately diplomatic relations when they address the illicit activity issues of counterfeiting our currency, counterfeiting pharmaceuticals, counterfeiting cigarettes, and trafficking in methamphetamine, when there is transparency and progress on the human rights issues, then we would talk about diplomatic relations. So it was not a sine qua non that with denuclearization comes normalization. No. We need denuclearization and that is a process toward normalization. But in that process, they get all those other aspects to economic benefits, and hopefully that would be enough of an inducement. And the North Koreans signed up to the 2005 joint statement.

Also in the 2005 joint statement is the provision of a light water reactor. When North Korea comes back to the NPT as a nonnuclear weapons state, because as North Korea said, they have a right to a civil nuclear program—and that is in there. And that was it.

And that fell apart because on the same day, the 19th of September, the North Koreans were offended by the fact that we had Banco Delta Asia. And that was a question asked this morning also. Banco Delta Asia—the predicate there was the Patriot Act, section 311, the predicate being money laundering. And North Koreans, using the Banco Delta Asia, were laundering their money. The Macao authorities retained $25 million of the money that North Korea had in this bank until the bank was in compliance with U.S. law and regulations.

Eventually the bank was in compliance. The money was returned to North Korea and I might add that it was returned through our own banking system, our financial institutions, because the North

Koreans insisted at that time they wanted to get into the international financial market and they wanted legitimacy.

But that got us back on the path to denuclearization. That was what the game was all about: denuclearization. We eventually took them off the list of state sponsors of terrorism, and that was to be in response to North Korea committing to a verification regime, that moves us toward comprehensive, verifiable, irreversible dismantlement of all their nuclear programs. They refused to sign a verification protocol, and that led to the unraveling of the September 2005 joint statement.

And that is unfortunate; it has gone downhill ever since: the 2006 and 2009 nuclear tests and missile launches, what we have just seen in 2012, and now what we have just seen last month in February with the third nuclear test. So North Korea is enhancing their nuclear capabilities and enhancing their missile capabilities.

The one point I will put on the table is that in April 2003, China brought North Korea to the table after they held back on some fuel that went into North Korea; it certainly was a message to North Korea to come, we want you at the table. In April 2003, China brought the United States and the North Koreans together, with China in the chair, and that was the beginning of the six-party process.

My personal view is China can do the same thing now. We bring South Korea into that process and sit down with North Korea and say, "What are you doing?" Is Kim Jong-un as committed to denuclearization and the joint statement as his father was? And get it on the record and address it and determine if there is any viability in the six-party process to go back to the September 2005 joint statement. I think that is a process. I think that is a meaningful one.

And I might add, as my last comment, that I was one of the few in early 2012 who was guardedly optimistic because I saw some personnel moves being made by Kim Jong-un coming into power. He replaced his Minister of Defense. He replaced the KPA, the chief of staff; he put a party officer who was overseeing the military as the director of the general political department; he brought his uncle into a very high position, so there was a momentum. And that all fell apart. After the Leap Day Agreement, they launched missiles and they have had a nuclear test. That has come to this position right now where we are at a stalemate, a very dangerous one.

And I think the Chinese now can really move this process forward, get us off the dime, get North Korea to the table, and get some momentum going here rather than continued escalation and a potential for confrontation.

[The prepared statement of Ambassador DeTrani follows:]

PREPARED STATEMENT OF AMBASSADOR JOSEPH R. DETRANI

From 2003 to 2006 I was the Special Envoy for Six-Party Talks (6PT) with North Korea and the U.S. Representative to the Korea Energy Development Organization (KEDO). For the following 4 years I was the North Korea Mission Manager with the ODNI; and from 2010 to 2012, I was the Director of the National Counterproliferation Center. Thus for the past 10 years, I have been intimately involved with developments in North Korea.

In 2004, during one of the first bilateral meetings we had with North Korea, during a plenary session of the 6PT in Beijing, the North Korean representative stated that if the 6PT process was unable to produce an acceptable agreement, North Korea would build more nuclear weapons, test these nuclear weapons and consider selling nuclear technology. We stated clearly that there would be severe consequences if North Korea pursued such an agenda. In this and subsequent bilateral meetings, during scheduled plenary sessions, the North Korean representative often stated that the United States should accept North Korea as a nuclear weapons state, noting that North Korea would be a responsible nuclear weapons state. The North Korean representative was told that U.S. policy was clear: complete, verifiable, irreversible dismantlement (CVID) of North Korea's nuclear programs was and will always be U.S. policy. During these bilateral sessions, we told the North Korean representative that comprehensive denuclearization would permit North Korea to receive economic assistance and security assurances, and once North Korea ceased its illicit activities—counterfeiting the U.S. $100 bill, counterfeiting cigarettes and pharmaceuticals, trafficking in methamphetamines—and started to address its human rights violations in a transparent manner, diplomatic relations would be possible.

With this as background, it's clear that there has been no progress in resolving North Korea's nuclear issue. In September 2005, there was hope that these issues with North Korea could be resolved, when the six countries agreed to a Joint Statement committing North Korea to comprehensive denuclearization in exchange for security assurances; economic assistance; and when North Korea returned to the NPT as a nonnuclear weapons state, the discussion of the provision of a light water reactor. Kim Jong-il had personally endorsed this agreement and on numerous occasions, to include during a visit to Beijing, stated his willingness to dismantle North Korea's nuclear programs. This optimism was dashed, however, when North Korea refused to commit to a written verification protocol to monitor North Korea's nuclear dismantlement efforts, after the United States removed North Korea from the list of state sponsors of terrorism.

Since the beginning of the 6PT process in 2003, North Korea has conducted three nuclear tests and four long-range ballistic missile launches, all in violation of U.N. Security Council resolutions. Prior to the 6PT process, starting in the mid-1990s, North Korea embarked on a clandestine uranium enrichment program, in violation of NPT obligations and counter to the intent and spirit of the 1994 Agreed Framework. North Korea had denied having a uranium enrichment program but in 2010 they permitted a visiting U.S. scientist to visit a sophisticated uranium enrichment facility in Yongbyon. Although North Korea maintained that their uranium enrichment program was for civilian purposes and fuel for the light water reactor they were building, the U.S. assessment was that this facility and other nondisclosed uranium enrichment facilities in North Korea were for the manufacture of highly enriched uranium (HEU), for nuclear weapons. This permitted North Korea to have two paths to fabricating nuclear weapons—Plutonium and HEU.

In addition to enhancing their long-range missile capabilities and their nuclear weapons programs, North Korea proliferated nuclear technology when they helped Syria build a nuclear weapons plutonium facility, similar to their 5 megawatt reactor in Yongbyon. This clandestine program started (ca. 1997) in Al Kibar, Syria. In 2007, just prior to going operational, Israel bombed and destroyed the facility. Additionally, North Korea has sold missiles and missile technology to Iran, Syria, Libya and any other country willing to buy their missiles.

Given North Korea's successful long-range missile launch in December 2012 that put a small satellite in orbit, and the February 2013 nuclear test that was larger than two previous tests, it appears that North Korea's objective is to fabricate smaller nuclear weapons that eventually can be mated to ballistic missiles that could reach the continental United States.

The three U.N. Security Council resolutions sanctioning North Korea for their nuclear tests and missile launches are causing considerable pain to the leadership in North Korea. The North Korean economy is barely functioning, with Pyongyang dependent on China for trade, fuel, and food assistance needed to sustain the government. Despite North Korea's significant economic problems, the Pyongyang government continues to spend billions of dollars on their nuclear and missile programs, under the banner of the "military first" policy.

If North Korea refuses to return to the 6PT and refuses to denuclearize, while enhancing their nuclear weapons and missile capabilities, other countries in east Asia most likely will consider having their own nuclear weapons capabilities. Indeed, the biggest threat globally, if North Korea retains its nuclear weapons, is nuclear proliferation. The possibility that nuclear weapons and/or nuclear materials is obtained by a rogue state or nonstate actors is of great concern. This message has been passed to the leadership in Pyongyang on numerous occasions.

Hopefully, China can help to convince the leadership in Pyongyang that the current escalatory path North Korea is pursuing will be disastrous for North Korea, the region and the international community. A potential nuclear arms race with the possibility of nuclear materials being acquired by terrorists and others will make the region and the world less secure. China is an ally of a North Korea that needs China's economic assistance. With the new leadership in Beijing, it's possible China will be able to convince Kim Jong-un to return to the 6PT and commit to eventual denuclearization, in line with the September 2005 Joint Statement. Kim Jong-il made this commitment. Hopefully, Kim Jong-un will.

Indeed, when Kim Jong-un succeeded his father last year, there was hope that this young leader would move North Korea in a positive direction and pursue denuclearization in return for international legitimacy and economic and security assurances. His first few months in power gave a number of us some optimism that the young Kim would move cautiously toward economic and political reform. He replaced many of the hard-liners in the government and appointed a Korean People's Party official as the Army's Chief of the General Political Department, thus installing a Party official to oversee the military. Other appointments, like the elevation of his Uncle to a more prominent position in government, gave some of us a sense of optimism; a sense that realists would replace the hard-liners. This appearance of liberalization was short-lived, however, when North Korea launched a TD–2 missile in April 2012, despite the February 29, 2012, Leap Day agreement with the United States that committed North Korea to a moratorium on missile launches and nuclear tests in return for nutritional assistance. U.N. sanctions then followed, with North Korea defiantly launching another missile in December 2012 that succeeded in putting a satellite in orbit. This also resulted in additional sanctions, with North Korea then conducting its third nuclear test last month. With this considerable escalation were vitriolic statements from Pyongyang stating that North Korea would never give up its nuclear weapons, claiming the United States maintains a hostile policy toward North Korea. It is likely North Korea will launch additional missiles and conduct additional nuclear tests, working toward smaller nuclear weapons with the hope of eventually being able to mate these nuclear weapons to missiles that can reach the United States. In short, North Korea has escalated tension significantly over the last year.

A negotiated settlement of North Korea's nuclear programs is desirable and necessary. My personal view is that China should do what they did in April 2003 when they convened an emergency meeting of the United States, North Korea, and China to discuss the tension in the region and arrange for the 6PT process to be established, to defuse tension and hopefully resolve the extant issues. It is possible that China could convene another emergency meeting with North Korea and the United States, that also includes South Korea. Such a meeting possibly could determine if North Korea is serious about eventual denuclearization for economic assistance and security assurances, pursuant to the September 2005 Joint Statement, and if reconvening the 6PT process is viable.

The CHAIRMAN. Thank you.
Ambassador Joseph.

STATEMENT OF HON. ROBERT G. JOSEPH, SENIOR SCHOLAR, NATIONAL INSTITUTE FOR PUBLIC POLICY, WASHINGTON, DC

Ambassador JOSEPH. Mr. Chairman, Senator Corker, thank you very much for the invitation to be here today and to testify. I will try to be very brief in summarizing my statement.

While one can argue and I think somewhat legitimately that U.S. policies have succeeded in slowing the North's progress and in galvanizing international support, the successes that we have reached, that we have achieved are at best tactical. As President John Adams once said, the facts are stubborn things. And today North Korea has declared itself to be a nuclear power and seems absolutely determined and well on its way to acquire the means to hold American cities hostage to their long-range missiles and nuclear weapons.

Viewing policy from a nonproliferation perspective, I see a long pattern of failed policies that must be changed. This change should be based on experience, not on hope, and it is on this basis that I offer the following lessons learned from my own experience.

One, North Korea will only agree to abandon its missile and nuclear programs if it is judged essential for regime survival. The DPRK places the highest values on these capabilities. These are a deterrent against attack. These are a means of preventing intervention such as occurred in Libya. Missile and nuclear programs are important to intimidate neighbors, to build prestige at home, to earn hard currency. In addition, the North has successfully used its nuclear program to attract inducements from those who seek its elimination.

Two, the prospect for a negotiated solution should be seen as a long shot. At times, previous administrations have thought they were all but there, but it never happened whether it was in 1992, in 1994, or in 2005. Pyongyang would formally agree to abandon its nuclear program only to violate its commitments each time. And this pattern of failed negotiations, followed by violations of obligations, provocations, and the offering of more inducements in turn by the United States and others to get North Korea back to the negotiating table, has been the main characteristic of U.S. policy for two decades.

The United States and others have and will, no doubt, continue to apply sanctions on the North, but imposing economic hardships and threatening isolation have not altered the regime's behavior. In part, this is because the DPRK cares little whether its people starve. In part, it is because regime stability is, in fact, dependent on isolation. In part, it is because China has continued to keep open a lifeline of assistance to the North no matter how blatant or how lethal its activities. And in part, it is because of our own practice of releasing pressure on North Korea in exchange for empty promises.

Three, the record of failed negotiations is not an argument that diplomacy should be abandoned. But negotiations by themselves is not a strategy. A comprehensive approach that integrates all tools of statecraft is required if negotiations are to have any chance of success. These tools, financial, intelligence, interdiction, law enforcement, and diplomacy—and we have talked about them all this morning—must be brought together to bring sustained pressure on the regime. Pyongyang must be faced with a choice: it can retain its missile and nuclear programs or it pays a high price. It must no longer be allowed to use these programs as a means to extract concessions that only serve to strengthen the regime and perpetuate the missile and nuclear threat. As for diplomacy, our main focus should be on China, the principal obstacle to bringing effective pressure on North Korea.

Four, the promotion of human rights, while part of official U.S. talking points for years, has not been a significant element of U.S. strategy. It should be as it was in the Reagan administration in its dealings with the Soviet Union. Exposing the domestic brutality of the regime is both the moral course and potentially an effective means to influence DPRK leaders.

Five, because North Korea is likely to retain its missile and nuclear capabilities, the United States must ensure that it can deter and defend against the threat. This requires missile defenses that protect allies and the U.S. homeland from attack. Failing to deploy defenses that keep pace with the growing threat, whether as a means to encourage Russian participation in offensive arms reductions or as a way to reduce the budget, will only undermine deterrence and increase the risk of destruction to the United States.

Similarly, we must continue to deploy a credible nuclear force that can meet the spectrum of deterrence requirements and provide solid assurance to allies. Going to lower and lower levels of forces in pursuit of a nuclear-free world is likely only to embolden our adversaries and shake the confidence of our friends and allies. And if our allies doubt our capacity or will to meet their security commitments, the outcome will be the reverse of the goal sought by global zero proponents: more rather than fewer nuclear weapons.

Six and finally, the last lesson is that the United States must lead. At times we have failed to show the required leadership, avoiding confrontation with the DPRK on a number of its most harmful activities, including its missile and nuclear proliferation. This absence of leadership affects not only the calculations in Pyongyang but also of Tehran where another oppressive regime is seeking missile and nuclear capabilities to undermine U.S. interests in a region of vital interest.

Iran does watch closely United States policy and United States resolve to reverse what three Presidents, President Clinton, President Bush, and now President Obama, have declared to be unacceptable: a nuclear-armed North Korea. What they have seen so far has certainly not dissuaded them.

Thank you again for the invitation of being here today. I look forward to your questions.

[The prepared statement of Ambassador Joseph follows:]

PREPARED STATEMENT OF DR. ROBERT G. JOSEPH

Chairman Menendez, Senator Corker, other distinguished members present today, thank you for the invitation to testify before the committee on the subject of U.S. policy toward North Korea. It is a privilege for me to appear again before this committee and provide my views and recommendations on the DPRK's missile and nuclear programs.

For the past 20 years, I have worked both in and out of government on fashioning and implementing policies to meet the threat that North Korea poses to the United States, to our friends and allies in the region, and to the broader international community. The nature and scale of this threat are most clearly reflected in Pyongyang's determined pursuit of longer range ballistic missiles and nuclear weapons. The DPRK satellite launch this past December, which involved much of the same technology as a missile test, and last month's nuclear test demonstrate the failure of U.S. policy approaches across three Presidential administrations. President Clinton, President Bush, and now President Obama, have all declared a nuclear-armed North Korea to be unacceptable. But all have watched as the North has developed and expanded these very capabilities.

While some may argue that U.S. policies have been successful in slowing the North's progress and in galvanizing support within the broader international community, such as witnessed in the adoption of U.N. Security Council resolutions imposing sanctions on the Kim regime, these successes are at best tactical. Today, North Korea has declared itself to be a nuclear power and appears determined to acquire the means to hold hostage American cities and American lives. Its neighbors, especially our allies Japan and South Korea, are currently within range of its short and medium range missiles, as are U.S. troops and bases in those countries. And the regime's history of selling both missile and nuclear technology, including to Iran and Syria, make the DPRK the number one proliferation threat of our time.

For these reasons, as one who assesses the strategic challenge from North Korea from the perspective of non- and counter-proliferation, I see a long-held pattern of failed policies that must be changed. The North Korea Nonproliferation and Accountability Act (S. 298), recently passed by the Senate, is a positive step. But more than a comprehensive report is necessary. The Obama administration should alter the familiar but futile course that has been followed by it and its two predecessors, Democrat and Republican alike. A new comprehensive strategy is required, based on experience not hope.

It is in this context that I offer the following lessons learned for your consideration.

(1) The Kim regime, now in its third generation, will agree to abandon its missile and nuclear programs only if it judges that such a move is essential for its survival. The DPRK places the highest value on its missile and nuclear capabilities, perhaps second only to the survival of the regime and keeping the elites loyal to sustain it. Nuclear weapons and ballistic missiles are seen as a deterrent to attack and as a means of preventing external interventions as occurred in Libya. Recent comments in the state-controlled media about the fate of Colonel Qadaffi after giving up his nuclear program reflect both the insecurities of the regime and its determination to keep its nuclear weapons. Missile and nuclear capabilities are also seen as important both to intimidate and coerce adversaries and to engender internal prestige at home.

The missile and nuclear programs are also a means of earning hard currency for a country that is economically bankrupt, as observed in sales of SCUD missiles to any customer with the ability to pay cash and the provision of a plutonium generating reactor to Syria. And, in both bilateral and multilateral negotiations, the North has used the nuclear program as a means of extracting inducements from the United States and others who seek its elimination, from heavy fuel oil to food assistance.

(2) Following from the first lesson, the prospect for a negotiated solution eliminating the North's missile and nuclear programs should be seen as a long shot. At times, previous administrations thought they were close to achieving this outcome, but it never happened. In the 1992 North-South Denuclearization Joint Declaration, in the 1994 Agreed Framework, and in the 2005 Six-Party Joint Statement, Pyongyang formally agreed to abandon its nuclear program, only to violate its obligations each time. In between agreements, expectations would rise and fall as the DPRK would pocket each successive concession, always demanding more.

This pattern of failed negotiations, each time followed by violations of commitments, provocations, and the offering of more inducements to get North Korea to return to the negotiating table, has been for two decades the main characteristic of U.S. policy toward North Korea. While the United States and others have at times applied sanctions on the North, such as after its missile and nuclear tests, these sanctions have not dissuaded the Kim leadership. Imposing economic hardships and threatening further isolation of the regime have not altered its behavior. In part, this is because the regime cares little whether all of its people are fed or starve, and prefers to keep them dependent on the state for their very existence. In part, it is because regime stability is dependent on its isolation. And in part, it is because China has undercut the impact of sanctions and has continued to keep open a lifeline of assistance to the North, no matter how blatant or lethal its actions.

(3) The record of failed negotiations is not an argument that diplomacy is hopeless, or that negotiations should be abandoned. But diplomacy as practiced in the past and present context does not constitute a strategy, even though it has most often masqueraded as such. A comprehensive approach that integrates all tools of statecraft is required if negotiations are to have any chance of succeeding and, alternatively, if we are going to be prepared to meet the threat if the DPRK continues its missile and nuclear proliferation activities.

Without such a change in U.S. policy, negotiations will not succeed. Specifically, Pyongyang must be faced with a choice: it can retain its missile and nuclear programs or pay a high price. It must no longer be allowed to use these programs as a means to extract concessions that only serve to strengthen the regime and perpetuate the missile and nuclear threat.

Pressure can have an effect on the regime's calculations. From 2001 through 2006, the United States employed a series of counterproliferation tools, including interdiction through the Proliferation Security Initiative, freezing regime funds abroad, and curtailing its illicit activities, such as cutting off its customer base for missiles and cooperating with other countries to end its drug and counterfeiting activities. These tools—financial, intelligence, law enforcement and diplomatic—must be brought together as part of a broader strategy for countering the North Korean threat. As for diplomacy, we need to move beyond diplomacy focused primarily on negotiating tactics or on the "carrots" for the next round of six-party or bilateral discussions. The main diplomatic focus should be on China, the principal obstacle to bringing effective pressure on the North.

(4) The promotion of human rights should be a major element of the U.S. strategy toward North Korea, as it was in the Reagan administration in its dealings with the Soviet Union. Exposing the North's brutality toward its own citizens has not been a priority component of U.S. policy. In fact, concerns about how such exposure might affect the prospects for engagement with the regime have worked to place human rights atrocities in a separate box which is mostly neglected if seen as complicating higher order diplomacy.

In North Korea, civil and religious freedoms do not exist. Political prison camps are reported to hold as many as 200,000 who have offended the regime and who suffer the greatest depravation, including summary executions and starvation. As with other totalitarian governments that lack moral legitimacy, the greatest fear of the rulers in Pyongyang is their own people, the foremost victims of their economic malfeasance and repression. Exposing the domestic crimes of the regime is both the moral course and, potentially, an effective means to influence DPRK leaders. Shining the spotlight on the darker corners of North Korea may also help strengthen international resolve to deal effectively with Pyongyang. The decision of the new Park government in Seoul to support a U.N. Commission of Inquiry to investigate rights abuses in the North is a welcome move that should facilitate giving more prominence to human rights issues by the United States.

(5) Because North Korea is likely to retain and expand its missile and nuclear capabilities, the United States must act to ensure that it can deter and defend against the threat. This requires missile defenses that can protect allies and the U.S. homeland from attack. Failing to deploy defenses that keep pace with the growing threat—whether as a means to encourage Russian participation in another round of offensive arms reductions or as a way to reduce the budget—will undermine deterrence and increase the risk of potentially immense destruction to the United States if deterrence fails. Yet, even as the North Korean threat grows, the Obama administration shows little interest in strengthening U.S. national missile defenses.

Similarly, the United States must continue to deploy a reliable and credible nuclear force that can meet the full spectrum of deterrence requirements and provide solid assurance to neighboring allies. Going to lower and lower levels of forces in the pursuit of a nuclear free world is likely to embolden our adversaries and shake the confidence of our friends. If U.S. allies doubt our capability or resolve to meet our security commitments in northeast Asia and elsewhere, the outcome will be the exact reverse of the stated goal of the proponents of global zero and minimal deterrence: more rather than less proliferation of nuclear weapons.

(6) The final lesson that I have learned related to U.S. North Korea policy is that the United States must lead if it is to succeed, either in negotiations, or in ensuring the needed capabilities for deterrence and defense, or in preventing the further spread of the North's deadly weapons of mass destruction. At times, the United States has failed to show the required leadership, avoiding confrontation with the DPRK on a number of its most harmful activities, including its missile and nuclear proliferation. This absence of leadership is recognized not just by the rulers in Pyongyang but by those in Teheran who also seek to acquire missile and nuclear capabilities to intimidate America's friends and undermine U.S. interests in another region of vital interest.

Iran, perhaps an even greater strategic threat than North Korea, watches closely U.S. policy and U.S. resolve in reversing what three Presidents have declared to be unacceptable: a nuclear-armed North Korea. What they have seen thus far has not dissuaded them from continuing down their path of nuclear proliferation.

Thank you again for the honor of appearing before the committee.

The CHAIRMAN. Thank you very much. Thank you all for your testimony.

Let us start and I would like to have an interplay between Ambassador Bosworth and DeTrani on this. If the 2005 joint statement was the best pathway toward achieving our goals—and, Ambassador DeTrani, you suggested that that issue, the Patriot Act sanctions of the bank and the $25 million that ultimately flowed back to North Korea was a disruptive element in pursuing the 2005 process. Clearly in any such process, there are going to be bumps along the road. Does that not really call into question how serious North Korea was even in this more expanded process of 2005 to achieving its goals? I would like both of your observations on that because it sounds to me that especially when the money ultimately flowed back to North Korea, that the process would have resumed again if there was a real desire to pursue it.

Ambassador DETRANI. No, Mr. Chairman. You are absolutely right. My point on the 2005 and the Banco Delta Asia was that we told the North Koreans very clearly that illicit activities would not be permitted. Diplomacy is one thing, and that is the 2005 joint statement on denuclearization. They continued to counterfeit our currency. They continued to deal with the methamphetamine and traffic in methamphetamine and counterfeit pharmaceuticals and so forth. That is law enforcement, and we told them we would continue to go after them on that. So they should not marry that up to diplomacy. These are two separate entities. And in fact, it was done on the same day, the 19th of September, when the Federal Register put out that the Banco Delta Asia was being sanctioned because of the predicate of money laundering based on section 311 of the Patriot Act. That was our message to the North Koreans; they cannot link the two and try to get us to go soft on illicit and human rights and put out denuclearization as the carrot for us to go on.

The CHAIRMAN. Evidently, while that may have been our message, they did not accept that message as a means to move forward.

Ambassador DETRANI. They protested and they walked away from the table for about 8 months until that money was returned. But, of course, the Banco Delta Asia was in compliance. So they were permitted legally to return that money.

The CHAIRMAN. Ambassador Bosworth, if that is the case it is so easily disrupted, how do we see that as the pathway forward?

Ambassador BOSWORTH. It is easily disrupted. As we have seen, North Korea's adherence to any of these agreements is tenuous at best, and they have to be continually reassured that they are not giving up their one piece of negotiating leverage in return for empty promises.

So I think it is very important, as we try to move forward, that North Korea come away with some conviction that it is not just denuclearization that we are going to make progress on. We are also going to try to make progress on a peace treaty to replace the armistice. And that I think is a very high priority from a North Korean point of view, as well, of course, as the diplomatic relations and economic assistance and energy assistance.

But please understand me. I am not saying that this is somehow a magic solution to the problem, but it is the one piece that we still have that they have agreed to and has constituted a foundation for trying to move forward. And they have not disavowed it in that sense.

The CHAIRMAN. Ambassador DeTrani, there are some press reports that suggest you have been on two secret missions to North Korea. And I am wondering if you could tell us what was the temperature of the interlocutors that you met with.

Ambassador DETRANI. Mr. Chairman, with due respect, sir, those reports have been addressed to the Senate and the House intelligence oversight committees, and I am really not at liberty to be discussing it here.

The CHAIRMAN. So you have discussed those with the House and Senate——

Ambassador DETRANI. The House and Senate intelligence oversight committees have been addressed. These issues have been addressed with these committees.

The CHAIRMAN. All right. So we will pursue it with the Intelligence Committee.

Let me ask you with reference to your comment that the Chinese were the ones who got the North Koreans to the table in 2005 as a result of tweaking them with some of their assistance. What was the calculus at that moment that made them do that, and how do we get them to make that calculus now?

Ambassador DETRANI. Sir, April 2003 was a very tense time. North Korea said they were reprocessing the spent fuel rods. They had pulled out of the NPT. They had asked the IAEA monitors to leave the country. It was very tense at that moment. Again, they left the NPT and asked the monitors to leave in January 2003. And then in April, they announced—even before April—in March they announced they were reprocessing the spent fuel rods that were in the cooling ponds at Yongbyon with the indication that they were going to be reprocessed for the purpose of weaponization. And it was tense. And the Chinese asked that the North Koreans come to the table with the United States and Beijing to speak about a way forward, to diffuse this very tense situation.

The reporting is that a number of days prior to those meetings, there were a few shipments of petroleum not sent to North Korea; shipments were not as extensive as they were in the past between the two countries. That was the reporting at the time. And the sense of some analysts at the time was that it could have been a message from Beijing to the DPRK that they should comply, and if they are being asked to sit at the table, they should sit at the table.

The CHAIRMAN. All right.

Senator Corker.

Senator CORKER. Thank you, Mr. Chairman.

And thank each of you for your testimony and for your past efforts regarding this issue.

It does not sound particularly hopeful to me, as I listen to each of you, and I think you would agree with that.

Let me just ask this question. We had some discussions here about our Libya intervention. Here we had a person that was equally not a good person. We had a person who had done away with weapons of mass destruction. We had a person that was working with us with al-Qaeda, and we took him out when they did not have weapons of mass destruction.

What kind of learning moment was that for, do you think, the leadership of North Korea?

Ambassador BOSWORTH. Well, I suspect they took away lessons from that that were inevitable and that are going to complicate our policymaking with them for the foreseeable future. The most obvious lesson would be if people think you have weapons of mass destruction and then you take action to show that you do not have weapons of mass destruction, this gives your adversaries room for maneuver that they might not have had previously. And there are, I think, legitimate reports that the North Koreans came away from both Iraq and Libya with the conviction that if these two countries had, in fact, had weapons of mass destruction, that what happened to them would not have happened to them.

Senator CORKER. Any other comments? There was a point I was trying to make at the time, but go ahead.

Ambassador DETRANI. Sir, I would agree. I think that the message in Pyongyang is that they saw what happened to Qaddafi and Saddam and so forth. It does not mean it is not doable in North Korea; that we will not succeed with denuclearization, but indeed, that fortified the hard-liners who were saying we just do not want to move down this path. There are those hard-liners in Pyongyang who are committed to retaining those nuclear weapons.

Senator CORKER. So I would just listen to earlier statements. Again, I do not see any real—I cannot imagine why North Korea would ever consider not going down the path they are going because of recent experiences. And it does not sound like to me that we have much of a way to deter that. I have not heard anybody speak to how we really do that other than China. It sounds like they are the only ones that have any cards that are worth playing here other than something that I think our country really does not want to engage in at this time. So it seems to me that the entire issue around North Korea really is not us but China. And I wonder if you might speak to that.

Ambassador DETRANI. Sir, I would just comment. I look to my colleagues, but it is a failed economy. I mean, North Korea, now with the additional sanctions—there are three sanctions in play now with this morning's—there are four sanctions, the U.N. sanctions. There are executive orders from our Treasury Department. They are biting and they have consequences. One would have to assume that when the leadership realizes they are not getting the funds necessary to sustain their lifestyle, the pressure will be at an even higher level even while provinces are not really seeing many benefits because of the two-state system. It is Pyongyang and the rest of the country. Once Pyongyang feels they are under siege and they are having problems sustaining it, I would imagine there would be some pressure on the leadership to make some changes to take some of that pressure off. And to live as a pariah state, especially if China is not happy with this pariah state, although they are allied with it, one has to wonder how they could survive in the near to midterm.

Senator CORKER. Ambassador.

Ambassador JOSEPH. Senator, I think that is a very important question. There is only one time in my experience in which I observed the Chinese on the cusp of making a strategic decision to change its relationship with North Korea, and that was in October 2006 after the first test. The first nuclear test was a profound shock. It was a profound shock in the region and it was internationally, given the risk to the nonproliferation regime itself.

Within a couple days of that test, Condi Rice was asked to go the region and asked me to go with her. We stopped in Japan. And in Japan, the focus of Prime Minister Abe, Foreign Minister Aso, was on the reassurance of the Japanese public that the United States would stand by its security commitments and explicitly restate its nuclear guarantee to Japan.

What is interesting is when we got to Beijing, the first thing the Chinese did was thank us for reaffirming our security and our nuclear guarantees to Japan. What China was concerned about was the nuclear dynamic. It was the dynamic of the possibility of Japan and maybe South Korea going nuclear in that context. That was the only time that there seemed to be a prospect, a window of opportunity for getting China to change its policy. This is the first time that China went along with the U.N. Security Council resolution which had real sanctions, 1718. China offered to work with us to implement those sanctions, including denying the luxury goods for the elites of North Korea.

But it was not too long after that that China went right back to its comfort zone and did not challenge the North Korean provocations. And it did that in the context of the United States and others releasing pressure on North Korea. Instead of increasing pressure, we released pressure. And we did that because of the false prospect of negotiations, the false promise that North Korea would come back to the negotiating table. And it did. And it did only to start, once again, the cycle of no negotiations, provocations, concessions, and failure to live up to its obligations.

I do not know what it is going to take to get China to change its assessment. China has many reasons for supporting North Korea. I mean, it is concerned about what happens with unification. It is concerned about refugees coming over the border.

It is going to take a real concerted effort, and quite frankly, it is going to take pressure on the part of the United States on China to change. More dialogue about the six-party talks is not going to do it. We are going to have to decide whether this is important enough to us that we actually put some pressure on China to change its policy.

But even if China changes its policy, I think that will be a very important step toward getting North Korea to alter course, but that is not enough either. We need a comprehensive strategy to deal with this.

The CHAIRMAN. Thank you.

Senator Murphy.

Senator MURPHY. Thank you, Mr. Chairman.

Ambassador Joseph, let me just follow up on that very important point. I asked a version of this question to Special Representative Davies.

I tend to agree that possibly the only thing that brings the Chinese to the table is the fear that there really does become a nuclear arms race in the region. And we sort of cavalierly throw around the inevitability of nuclear arms races in the Middle East and in that sector of the world as well without any, I think, true understanding of all of the barriers that would stand in the way of that happening, particularly in a place where we hold a lot of cards with the other players in the region.

So you maybe just answered this, but you talk about applying real pressure to China, but without China feeling that they lose control of the nuclear situation in the region, what cards do we have to play there?

And I guess the second question is, Is there any chance that we do lose control of the nuclear capabilities of the region? Is there any real chance that the Japanese and the South Koreans do change their disposition and decide to remove themselves from our nuclear umbrella and develop their own capacities, or is that not realistic?

Ambassador JOSEPH. Senator, taking your second question first, I think there is a chance that if we fail with North Korea and if we do not demonstrate through both our declaratory policy and our capacity in both the nuclear area, as well as in the missile defense area, there is a likelihood that Japan will overcome its long-term allergy about nuclear weapons and begin to hedge. South Korea also very much a concern about proliferation in the future if we fail—if we fail—with North Korea.

In terms of what cards we have to play with China, there are not any easy ones. If there were easy ones, I think we would have played them by now. This has been going on for 20 years. I think we have to make the assessment whether or not this issue—the issue of North Korea and China's continuing support, continuing lifeline of assistance to North Korea—is sufficiently important to us that we begin to put economic pressure on China, that we begin to call out China for its part in sustaining what is the most abhorrent regime I think in the world today. There are a number of things that we can do, but up until today, we have been more interested in China's role as a facilitator in the six-party talks. That does not get us to where we need to be with China.

Senator MURPHY. Let me ask sort of the same version of that question to the other two panelists. Do you agree that the thing that China fears most is the nuclear arms race, and what are your thoughts on whether that is a real concern?

Ambassador BOSWORTH. Well, I think China is concerned about proliferation within the region.

Senator MURPHY. Is that their primary concern?

Ambassador BOSWORTH. No. It is one of several concerns. They are also concerned about the stability of North Korea for the reasons that we spoke of earlier. They are also concerned about the nature of their relationship with the United States, and I think it has been made quite clear to them that while North Korea policy is not a pivot for that relationship, it is, nonetheless, very important to that relationship. So they have very many points of interest at play here.

And I think we sometimes make the mistake of thinking that China is somehow a policy monolith in which problems are fed and then solutions come out. One of the things that I came away from my recent experience dealing with this problem—or convinced of— is that the Chinese are of various minds about how to deal with North Korea. There is no single view, and it is something that is being very much debated and addressed within the policy circles of North Korea, both within the government, within the party, and within the so-called think-tank world. So they do not have a solution to these concerns. They recognize the nature of the problem. They recognize that it is something they have got to deal with, but they also understand how complicated and how many different points of interest in China are concerned about possible outcomes in North Korea. That includes the party, the military, and the government.

The CHAIRMAN. Thank you.

Senator Shaheen.

Senator SHAHEEN. Thank you, Mr. Chairman.

And thank you to all of the panelists for being here. I am sorry I missed the earlier part of the hearing but very much appreciate your insights into what is happening in North Korea now, especially you, Mr. Bosworth, and your New Hampshire connection through Dartmouth. So nice to welcome you here.

Ambassador BOSWORTH. Thank you.

Senator SHAHEEN. I wanted to follow up a little bit on the proliferation issues that have been raised because it seems to me that given the past history, given their efforts to help Syria build a nuclear weapons facility, that we may not know exactly what we do not know about what North Korea is doing with respect to proliferation efforts. And I just wondered how comfortable each of you are with where our knowledge of what is happening with respect to North Korea and proliferation might be right now and if you can elaborate on exactly what we know about that.

Ambassador DETRANI. Can I just comment very briefly? And I will look to my colleagues. My colleagues mentioned Syria and al-Kibar. That was in many ways a wake-up call. That was going on for a number of years, and until the Israelis took it out in September 2007, I mean, that was almost going operational. Nuclear proliferation is central to the whole issue of denuclearization for North Korea, and that drives China and everyone else, but certainly China, as a neighbor and an ally. If there is any instability there, what would happen with the nuclear weapons or the fissile materiel? So proliferation—and of course, we know the element of—the potential for nuclear terrorism there. There are nonstate actors out there that want their hands on this.

So this is a very central issue to why denuclearization for the DPRK has to be, if you will, the goal and objective. It is not nonproliferation. It is not arms control. It is denuclearization because of all of these other reasons, and proliferation is central to it.

Senator SHAHEEN. Anything either of you would like to add about what we know about those efforts?

Ambassador BOSWORTH. Well, I would only add, Senator, that as a longtime consumer of intelligence within the government, I have been impressed on the one hand by how hard our intelligence community works on North Korea, but I have also been impressed by what a difficult target North Korea is. And I think their capacity for surprise, while not limitless, is certainly greater than we might expect.

Senator SHAHEEN. Mr. Joseph.

Ambassador JOSEPH. Senator, I come at this from a nonproliferation perspective and that is my expertise, if I have expertise. And clearly, North Korea has, for decades, been the No. 1 proliferator. It is a serial proliferator. We know it from its missile sales and the transfer of missile technology to a number of countries. We know it from the Syria experience in providing a plutonium reactor to Syria. North Korea will sell what it has.

I am very concerned not only about state proliferation relationships but also, as Ambassador DeTrani just mentioned, the nonstate and access through North Korea to fissile material and weapons. And it is, as someone said, a very hard intelligence problem, and we have been subject to a number of strategic surprises in this area. So despite knowing how hard the intelligence community works on this problem, I also share the sense that there is a lot we simply do not know and we need to be prepared for the worst based on North Korea's experience.

Senator SHAHEEN. So you have dashed my hopes to be reassured.

As we enter another round of sanctions, how can we be more successful at implementing those sanctions in a way that really has a real impact on North Korea? Because my understanding is that to date we have had rather sporadic success at implementing the sanctions.

Ambassador BOSWORTH. I think we have to start with the realization of the reality, which is that sanctions by themselves are not going to solve this problem. Sanctions can make life even more difficult for North Korea. Sanctions can force North Korea to contemplate issues that they might not have contemplated without them. But sanctions are not the solution to this problem. It is part of the solution conceivably, but they are not the solution. Sanctions have the effect of making us confident that we are at least doing something, that we are not just sitting here passively and waiting for divine intervention of this problem. We are taking some action, but we should not, in my personal judgment, be under any illusions that sanctions are going to solve this problem.

Ambassador DETRANI. I would look to Ambassador Joseph, and I do not disagree with Ambassador Bosworth.

But I will say I think what we saw today with China, who is very much a part of this new U.N. Security Council resolution; I think it is indicative of the fact that China is also saying what is going on here. And I think we need to have all the countries coming together, whether it is a proliferation security initiative, whether it is going after the banking system, or whether it is going after their diplomats and how they move money and so forth, all of this is causing significant pain to North Korea.

Now, is that going to be the answer? Certainly that is not the answer per se, but it is part of the process to telling North Korea they must change their behavior. They need come back to the table and need to commit again, recommit to denuclearization.

Ambassador JOSEPH. Well, just to add to my colleague's comments with which I certainly agree, sanctions will only work—and I think they have limited impact—but they will only work in the context of a broader strategy. It is not a question of sanctions or our strategy or diplomacy as our strategy. We have got to put these various instruments together, and that has been lacking.

And what also has been lacking is a sustained effort. When we have made a difference, when we have created pain—and I think the Banco Delta Asia experience is very apt here. When we have put pressure on the North, we have allowed that pressure to be released. We have done that through this false and fanciful promise of negotiations. Negotiations will only work if we apply pressure, and that is one thing we learned from the Libyan experience. It was not you get into negotiations, you release the pressure. I mean, this is negotiating 101. And yet, time after time, Republican and Democratic administrations, we have made the same fundamental mistake with North Korea. A lot of it is because we hope. We hope North Korea will change, and we ignore our experience for the sake of hope.

Senator SHAHEEN. Thank you. I am out of time. I would love to follow up and see how that fits with what is being proposed on Iran, but that is a different topic.

Thank you all.

The CHAIRMAN. Well, thank you all for your very insightful comments and answers to questions on a very challenging but important national security and national interests issue before the committee and before our country.

So with the thanks of the committee, the committee's record will remain open until the close of business tomorrow.

And with that, the hearing is adjourned.

[Whereupon, at 12:23 p.m., the hearing was adjourned.]

ADDITIONAL MATERIAL SUBMITTED FOR THE RECORD

RESPONSES OF SPECIAL REPRESENTATIVE GLYN T. DAVIES TO QUESTIONS SUBMITTED BY SENATOR JEFF FLAKE

CHINA AND NORTH KOREA

Question. North Korea is dependent on China for economic aid and diplomatic support. North Korea's cycle of provocation followed by cooperation, and the numerous tests of missiles and nuclear devices, has led to several rounds of United Nations sanctions that China has supported. However, China has yet to agree to more stringent economic measures against North Korea outside the United Nations.

- What will it take to gain China's cooperation to rein in North Korea's provocative activities?
- The United States is working to gain China's cooperation on a number of other critical international issues such as Iran's nuclear weapons program and Syria's civil war. Where does North Korea fit in on that list? Is it a priority? If it is not, why isn't it?
- Is China in a position to bring the North Korean regime—and its nuclear weapons program—to its knees by withholding assistance to it?
- Does the Obama administration view the North Korean regime as a threat to U.S. national security?

Answer. The United States continues to work closely with China to address North Korea's nuclear programs and other provocations. We continue to concentrate our diplomatic energy on encouraging China to more effectively leverage its unique relationship with the DPRK and its role as chair of the six-party talks to achieve our common goal of verifiable denuclearization of the Korean Peninsula in a peaceful manner. The Chinese played a critical role in crafting U.N. Security Council Resolution 2094, which imposes new sanctions on North Korea, and we will continue to press China to enforce these tough new sanctions. We will also continue to press China to do everything possible to address North Korea's threats to regional peace and security and the global nonproliferation regime.

While the United States is working with China to address a number of critical international issues, including Iran's nuclear weapons program and the unrest in Syria, North Korea remains a top priority in our policy agenda with China. Secretary Kerry has already discussed our concerns regarding North Korea, including after North Korea's missile launch and after its nuclear test, with new State Councilor Yang Jiechi.

While China provides some assistance to North Korea, we are not in a position to speculate on the potential impact of withholding that assistance. Chinese officials have made clear that they are concerned by North Korea's destabilizing and provocative behavior, and that they view denuclearization of the Korean Peninsula as a critical concern.

North Korea's recent highly provocative threats against the United States and its allies and its announcement that it had tested a nuclear device in February underscore the serious threat the DPRK's nuclear weapons and ballistic missile programs and proliferation activities pose to U.S. national security and the security of our allies. The United States will continue to take appropriate action to counter these threats.

U.S. DISARMAMENT AND NORTH KOREA

Question. President Obama supports the denuclearization of the North Korean peninsula. There are some who have advocated for the United States to reduce its nuclear arsenal as a way of persuading other rogue regimes such as North Korea to give up their nuclear weapons as well. However, despite new reductions agreed to under the New START treaty, North Korea recently tested a nuclear device. During the hearing I asked you if reductions to the U.S. nuclear arsenal would persuade North Korea to give up its programs and come back to negotiations. Your response was that while it wouldn't have a direct effect on North Korea, it would have tremendous effect on the 189 countries who are party to the Nuclear Non-Proliferation Treaty, and that, in turn, would have an effect on North Korea.

- Would reductions to the U.S. arsenal prompt Japan and South Korea to develop nuclear weapons programs of their own?
- If Japan and South Korea did develop their own programs, how would that affect North Korea's proliferation activities?
- What would the effect be on proliferation in general if, while the United States reduced its stockpile, Japan and South Korea began to develop their own?

Answer. The Republic of Korea (ROK) and Japan are both committed partners and global leaders on strengthening and maintaining the integrity of the global nonproliferation regime. Both countries also stress their support for efforts by the nuclear weapon-state parties to the Treaty on the Non-Proliferation of Nuclear Weapons (NPT) to fulfill their treaty commitments on nuclear disarmament.

The 2010 Nuclear Posture Review (NPR) makes clear that the United States will maintain a safe, secure, and effective nuclear arsenal as long as nuclear weapons exist. The NPR effectively balances the need to demonstrate progress toward meeting our commitments under the NPT and maintaining our security commitments and a credible extended nuclear deterrence to our allies and partners, including the ROK and Japan.

The U.S. nuclear umbrella, along with our robust conventional weapons capabilities, will remain sufficiently strong to assure the ROK and Japan of our defense commitment, including to a strong response to any threat from North Korea, even if the United States reduced its stockpile. The United States is strongly committed to the defense of our allies, the ROK and Japan, and we have seen no evidence that either Japan or the ROK intends to develop its own nuclear weapons program in response to a possible reduction to the U.S. nuclear arsenal.

RESPONSES OF SPECIAL REPRESENTATIVE GLYN T. DAVIES TO QUESTIONS SUBMITTED BY SENATOR BENJAMIN L. CARDIN

Question. North Korea on March 11 cut off the Red Cross communications hotline between Seoul and Pyongyang which was used for general communication and to discuss aid shipments and separated families' reunions. This has largely been seen as a symbolic gesture.

- When was the last time it was cut off? How did that impact our interactions with North Korea and our ability to respond to confrontation?
- What impact do we expect this latest cut-off to have, if any?
- Do we expect that Pyongyang will also follow up on threats to cut off a separate hotline with U.N. forces in South Korea, at the border "truce village" of Panmunjom? What would the outcome of that be? Has that ever been cut off before?

Answer. North Korea's reported cutoff of North-South Red Cross communication links at Panmunjom on March 11, 2013, is not conducive to ensuring peace and stability on the Korean Peninsula. The last time the DPRK Red Cross stopped answering the Red Cross hotline was on May 26, 2010, after the Republic of Korea (ROK) announced countermeasures in response to the sinking of an ROK Navy ship. Communications resumed on January 12, 2011.

North Korea has periodically refused to acknowledge the communications channel at Panmunjom, and its recent bellicose rhetoric and threats follow a pattern designed to raise tensions and intimidate others. North Korean forces at Panmunjom at times do not answer their phone line connecting to the United Nations (U.N.) Command. In the past, the impact of their refusal to answer the phone has been minimal and we do not anticipate any negative effect from this latest cutoff. The United States continues to have direct channels of communication with the DPRK unrelated to the hotline in Panmunjom and we will continue to draw upon the full range of our capabilities to protect against, and to respond to, the threat posed to us and to our allies by North Korea.

Question. What type of support is the United States Government currently providing for American nongovernmental organizations (NGOs) working in North Korea, if any?

• Which American NGOs are working in North Korea?
• How can we best get aid to them?
• How can we account for and track the aid?

Answer. The United States remains deeply concerned about the well-being of the people of North Korea and supports nongovernmental organization (NGO) activities by offering technical and other assistance. There are a handful of U.S.-based NGOs working in North Korea. These NGOs secure funds from a variety of sources, including, at times, very limited and strictly controlled funding from the U.S. Government.

U.S.-based NGOs are working in critical areas to improve the lives of North Koreans. U.S.-based NGO activity in North Korea includes providing medicine, medical equipment, and medical training; nutritional assistance to children in orphanages to help alleviate chronic undernutrition; agricultural assistance to improve farming methods in order to address critical food security issues; water and sanitation programs to fight waterborne disease; recovery assistance following flooding and other natural disasters; and other assistance targeted at North Korea's most vulnerable populations. The United States has not funded any nutrition assistance programs to the DPRK since March 2009. The Department of State has established rigorous controls and reporting requirements to ensure that any U.S.-funded support reaches its intended beneficiaries, and U.S. NGOs strictly follow these monitoring requirements. Other NGOs equip North Koreans with tools to improve the country's social, economic, and other frameworks, and facilitating cultural and other forms of exchanges. We monitor these NGO activities to be certain that they do not enhance North Korean capabilities that are under U.S. and U.N. sanctions.

Given the sensitivity of this work and concern for the security and safety for U.S. NGOs operating in North Korea, we cannot provide a comprehensive list of U.S. NGOs operating in North Korea in this setting, but would be pleased to provide more details on specific U.S. NGOs working in North Korea and specific monitoring requirements in a confidential briefing.

○